RELAX RELASE LET GO

The 8-Step Solution To Destroy Limiting Beliefs That Are Keeping You From Feeling Free, Whole And Happy

© Copyright 2017 by Paul Robbins & Susan Robbins - All rights reserved.

This document is geared towards providing exact and reliable information in regards to the topic and issue covered. The publication is sold with the idea that the publisher is not required to render accounting, officially permitted, or otherwise, qualified services. If advice is necessary, legal or professional, a practiced individual in the profession should be ordered.

- From a Declaration of Principles which was accepted and approved equally by a Committee of the American Bar Association and a Committee of Publishers and Associations.

In no way is it legal to reproduce, duplicate, or transmit any part of this document in either electronic means or in printed format. Recording of this publication is strictly prohibited and any storage of this document is not allowed unless with written permission from the publisher. All rights reserved.

The information provided herein is stated to be truthful and consistent, in that any liability, in terms of inattention or otherwise, by any usage or abuse of any policies, processes, or directions contained within is the solitary and utter responsibility of the recipient reader. Under no circumstances will any legal responsibility or blame be held against the publisher for any reparation, damages, or monetary loss due to the information herein, either directly or indirectly.

Respective authors own all copyrights not held by the publisher.

The information herein is offered for informational purposes solely, and is universal as so. The presentation of the information is without contract or any type of guarantee assurance.

The trademarks that are used are without any consent, and the publication of the trademark is without permission or backing by the trademark owner. All trademarks and brands within this book are for clarifying purposes only and are the owned by the owners themselves, not affiliated with this document.

Introduction

Dr. Paul Robbins is an author and behavioral coach on the application of emotional intelligence in everyday lives. He ran a coaching and counseling service in Singapore for 12 years, with his wife and business partner Susan Robbins, a pioneer in the field of personal development and human wellness, before establishing their private consultancy service, on the Gold Coast, Queensland, Australia in 2009.

Paul and Susan are committed to helping personal clients and corporate executives reduce their stress after an emotional event—empowering people to take ownership of their emotions for a more meaningful life.

Dr. Robbins provides a suite of coaching programs. He is accredited to administer three emotional intelligence psychometric tests and documents and measures stakeholder recognition and evaluation of long-term positive change in behavior of coaching clients to bring you a new level of self understanding and, most importantly, greater effectiveness in your life.

Susan is a valued and experienced cognitive-behavioral counselor and mental health social worker. She conducts an active professional confidential counseling practice for individuals, couples and corporate executives, specializing in relationship, anxiety, anger management, self esteem, grief & loss, trauma, adult ADD and emotional pain counseling.

Contents

Introduction 1

Chapter 1 Recognize The Stress Response— Survive Your Life Dramas 7
    1.1 Introduction 7
    1.2 Your Emotional Brain 8
    1.3 Autonomic Nervous System (ANS) 11
    1.4 Stress Felt In the Body 12
    1.5 What Stress Looks Like 16
    1.6 Symptoms of Stress 19
    1.7 Physical Effects Of Stress 23
    1.8 Psychological Effects Of Stress 24
    1.9 The Highly Sensitive Person (HSP) 26

Chapter 2 Know Your Emotional Style — How You Deal With Your Emotions 33
    2.1 Introduction 33
    2.2 Reactive and Avoidant Emotional Styles 34
    2.3 Who's to blame? 40
    2.4 Surviving Your Emotional Style 42

Chapter 3 Understand How You Generate Emotion — Get Smart At Noticing your Emotions 45
    3.1 Introduction 45
    3.2 Label Emotions 46
    3.3 Six Emotion Families 47
    3.4 EAR—Identity: The Person You Want To Be 48
    3.5 Use The Gap To Give My Life Meaning 51
    3.6 Understand Self Esteem 52
    3.7 Recognize Your Inner Voice 55
    3.8 The Breathing Square 60
    3.9 Unpack Your Negative Jigsaw 61
    3.10 4-Step Cognitive Framework 63
    3.11 Get Smart at Noticing Your Emotions 64

Chapter 4 Manage Your Emotional Pain — Emotional Awareness Means Owning And Taking Responsibility For Your Actions 66
    4.1 Introduction 66
    4.2 Develop Emotional Awareness 67
    4.3 Pain Perception and Arousal 70

4.4 From Anger to Assertion—Paul Robbins 74
4.5 From Fear to Appreciation Susan Robbins.. 79
4.6 Stress + Stress + Stress = Depression 83
4.7 Surviving Your Depression 84
4.8 Treatment for Depression... 88
4.9 To Medicate or Not to Medicate 89
4.10 Medication Myths.. 90

Chapter 5 Communicate Effectively — The Key to Any Relationship 95
5.1 Introduction 95
5.2 Active Listening 96
5.3 Communication Model 99
5.4 Helping Model of Communication Skills 100
5.5 X-Y-Z of Effective Communication 103
5.6 Communication Differences between Men And Women............... 105

Chapter 6 Manage The Emotion of Others — Recognizing, Knowing And Predicting Change 114
6.1 Introduction 114
6.2 First Manage Your Own Emotions 115
6.3 The Change Process 117
6.4 Distinguish Grief from Depression 124
6.5 Develop Emotional Knowledge 129
6.6 Be Exceptional at Empathizing... 131

Chapter 7 Reconnect And Reduce Your Stress — Get Your Relationships Back On Track.. 134
7.1 Introduction 134
7.2 Relationship Cycle 136
7.3 Indifference... 141
7.4 Unmet Expectations.. 147
7.5 Resolving Resentments 149
7.6 Handling Difficult People 152
7.7 Giving and Receiving Love... 155
7.8 Sandcastle of Trust.. 160
7.9 Trauma of betrayal 163

Chapter 8 Achieve Lasting Happiness — And Give Happiness To Others 166
8.1 Introduction 166
8.2 Emotion—The Force Of Real Life 167
8.3 Conclusion.. 168

Relax Release Let Go

Introduction

> *Relax Release Let Go* is a powerful body of knowledge that you can apply every day to reduce your stress after an emotional event.

Emotion; your emotion and the emotion of others. Everything you do in life is affected by emotion—what you feel. When you feel positive emotion, life is good. When you feel negative emotion, life is often bad.

In this book we will give you the most precious thing in life— *more time*.

More time will give you more of the things you want. You want to find fulfillment in sound relationships. Your deepest, most cherished desire is to be in a relationship where you are happy and secure, where you can be yourself, fulfilling your life goals with passion and purpose. You want to feel better, conquer, move on from and get through problems or difficult behavior without resentments and without a feeling of insecurity that you won't get through them. You want to increase your emotional well-being and peace of mind. You want to learn more about life and share your knowledge with others to help them. You want your children to avoid some of the mistakes that you, and others you know, have made.

By creating **more time** you can fulfill these needs and:

- feel good, not burdened or weighed down by resentments, fear and insecurity.
- minimize negative emotion (stress) and see that your problems are taken care of.
- increase emotional well-being and peace of mind, knowing you will 'get through'.

As you read this book you will start a process that will give you *more time* to feel GOOD about yourself and your relationships—a process that will make you feel safe. Know that good people are found in bad relationships. If you are hurting, stressed out or in a bad relationship, create time for yourself by making changes in your own behavior using the strategies found in this book. The process is ongoing, but the immediate benefit to you is that you will manage your emotions better, reduce your stress, and start to build healthy happy relationships.

Whether you are aware of it or not, all your behavior is governed by your feelings and your feelings are governed by your brain. The need to feel good is a primitive need. Feeling good means there is an absence of a bad feeling, an absence of stress. Feeling GOOD, at a primitive level, tells you that you are safe.

Personal choices can lead to prosperity or dereliction. Good choices are a non-problem status. Bad choices bring pain. Emotion matters because when you know how to reduce stress after an emotional event you can deliver a balance of good and bad feelings—you can manage the physical and psychological symptoms of stress that virtually keep you alive.

Each of has an irrepressible drive to be emotionally free, independent, and able to make responsible choices that do not impact adversely on ourselves, those whom we lover and cherish, and those with whom we work. We all want to give and receive love. We all want to get to a point in our relationships with others where there is nothing left unsaid between us. We all want to be free of fear, anxiety, bewilderment and withdrawal; free of irritation, frustration and anger; and free of avoidance of friends and family. This book shows you how.

But first, I want to share with you why emotion matters so much to me.

It was April 1974. I had arrived home to an empty apartment in Sydney, Australia. My wife had left our home and taken our twin daughters aged two with her. We had been married just four years. I was shocked! I felt devastated, confused, angry, alone, and full of despair. It was an overwhelming "Oh Shit!" experience.

Unbeknownst to me at the time, I was about to enter a period consumed by profound grief and loss that eventually set me on the path to creating a comprehensive system for behavior change, learning and applying my emotional intelligence, teaching others, writing this book and creating the world's largest online resource on emotional wealth—EmotionMatt.com

I tried desperately to reconcile my marriage. I spent hours alone, feeling suicidal; crying and pleading with her on the phone to reconsider her decision to leave. I was to learn that my former wife had not loved me for some time; we were just housemates. She was in fact scared of me. Scared of me! I was bewildered and indignant. At my core I was a good man with great principles, who loved my family beyond measure. Surely she knew that! Yet my drinking and occasional violent behavior, my irritable tones, and my unpredictability had caused her to be fearful of any future with me.

The decision of my former wife to leave was based on her perception—supported by the perceptions of her doctor at the time (who had never met me), government social welfare officials and friends and family—that I was a "write-off" and had no future. Was she right in leaving me and removing my young children from me? Was it in her and my children's best interests to leave the marriage? Were her family, doctor and the government officials right in their judgement of me at the time that I was "to blame" for the marriage breakdown and incapable of bringing up my young children? You the reader must judge that for yourself once you have read this book.

In my grief and self pity, I recalled that my former wife had asked me several times to go and see a counselor. It wasn't that I was against the idea; I simply had not gotten around to it. Soon after she left with our girls I was admitted by my doctor to the mental health wing of a hospital in Sydney and placed under benzodiazepine medication. During the day I was asked to participate in group discussions, which I came to realize later were for hospital staff to assess patients as to their mental and physical functioning. I was assessed as not having psychological problems and was released a couple of days later to get on with life after some good doses of valium to calm me. And I learned to manage the pain of divorce and separation from my children. But the experience motivated me to look at and change my behavior.

After I had moved to live and work in Adelaide in April 1974 to try and salvage my marriage, I had a wake-up call—what I call my "Oh, shit!" experience. I remember visiting with a social worker at the local Catholic Cathedral in Adelaide some months after our separation. I used to go to the Cathedral regularly to be still, pray and find peace with God. I would light a candle for each of my former wife and twin daughters and seek God's way forward. In counseling the social worker challenged me; "Paul, don't you know that heavy drinking and hitting your wife (which I did on one occasion) is not acceptable behavior?" I was shocked! At age 25 I was finally 'getting it'. I was beginning my journey of awareness.

As I grieved the loss of my first family, I would stand at the kitchen window in my upstairs flat at Henley Beach, Adelaide and look up at the beautiful Adelaide hills in the distance, praying that God would forgive me for the pain I had caused and provide me with a life partner whom I could love and feel loved by in return. In December 1975 I met Susan, who by chance sat beside me on a short flight from Port Lincoln to Adelaide, where we had both been for the day in our respective jobs. We married in 1977. Susan is the love of my life, business partner, confidant and friend, and as I write this, we have been together 36 years.

Susan and I have two wonderful sons, James and William. We lived in Adelaide for 20 years before moving to Singapore, where we conducted a hugely successful behavioral counseling and coaching practice for 12 years until the Global Financial Crisis caused us to close it in February, 2009. We have reconstructed our clinic on the Gold Coast, Queensland, Australia, where we now live. We feel privileged that in more than 14 years in private practice, we have helped thousands of people become extraordinary and helped bring clarity, purpose, happiness and abundance to their lives. This is our passion and the reason we were brought together.

Susan is a caring, supportive and compassionate person who has loved me constantly and provided overwhelming support for my career and varied business ventures over many years. Together we have faced highs and lows, including our own relationship difficulties and the closure of our Singapore business with severe fi losses. She embraced fully my former life circumstances, including my eldest daughter, who was born in 1969 from my relationship with my former wife before we married in 1970. My former wife and I had agreed to adopt her out at birth, and she as an adult took the initiative to search for and find her birth mother. To our great delight she connected with Susan and me in 2007.

Susan is a trained cognitive-behavioral counselor and mental health social worker, working in Australia and Singapore for more than 34 years. Our marriage is stable and will not collapse with sudden change. We deal skillfully with new situations and discuss and work on our marriage and different emotional styles each and every day to achieve the best outcomes.

Today, our organization, Robbins International, is nearly 15 years old, provides emotional counseling and coaching, is a producer of books and emotional development digital information products, and is building an online global community. Our organization and my marriage to Susan stand as testimony to my belief that emotion does matter. You can regain control over your emotions, change your behavior for the better, and be mindful of the impact of your own negative thinking on your body and on other people. Separation and divorce is not the only option.

> *Life is a series of events. Every event is an opportunity for change. And it is from the most painful events that you change the most.*

I have experienced several painful episodes in my life, but thankfully many happy events too. Losing my family in 1974 has been the most painful. Had it not happened I may not have met Susan and written this book. Emotion matters so much to me because with lots of hard work I have learned to make the necessary changes in my thinking to reduce my stress after emotional events. Each day I remind myself that I am married to an highly sensitive person and that I have work to do! I use the tools in this book to live each new day making responsible choices; taking responsibility for the impact of my choices on others. I invite you to join Susan and me on this journey to fi the keys to emotional health.

—Paul Robbins, Ph.D.

1
Recognize The Stress Response— Survive Your Life Dramas

1.1 Introduction

Imagine a zebra grazing in the long grass. It hears a sudden noise in the nearby trees and immediately it's off and running in the other direction. Once it has put some distance between itself and the noise it turns back to look and assess. It's just an antelope coming out to graze as well. Okay. There is no danger. The zebra looks around at whatever else may be lurking. Nothing. It walks back toward the patch of grass it was working on, but its ears are still twitching, its heart is still pounding. Eventually it will sett down.

In normal everyday life there is an optimal level of stress needed for alertness and clarity of thought, and for being on guard. We call this the stress response. To achieve this state, the brain generates and manages adrenalin, the chemical attached to the "fight or flight" response.

What happens when there is drama in your life? Whether these dramas (events) are emotional or physical, heightened levels of adrenalin from the increase in stress can affect your body, and consequently your mind, in serious ways.

Awareness of how every internal or external event in your life comes into your brain through the limbic system, which assesses all sensory experiences for threat or danger and determines your emotional style, will give you insight into how the emotion centre of your brain really works, and will help you elevate your emotional well-being. Zebras flee when they can, and fight if they must. Humans are more complicated.

1.2 Your Emotional Brain

Everything is about how you feel. Stress is the feeling of negative emotion in your body. The process of stress rising and falling in the body is biological—stress is triggered by, but can be minimized by, your emotional brain. Your senses connect you to the world around you through your emotional brain. Perception is the process by which information about the outside world impinges on the sensory organs and is then decoded and interpreted by the brain, resulting in a conscious experience—a behavior or response. Perception is one aspect of cognition, which encompasses all the mental activities that enable us to understand our environment and make decisions about it. When we perceive *emotion* we are receiving and interpreting information from both external (the world around us) and internal (the world inside us) environments.

There are four major regions of the brain; the brain stem, the cerebellum, the cortex (cerebrum) and the limbic system. The limbic system—comprising the thalamus, hypothalamus, hippocampus, amygdala, and connection pathways—mediates and expresses emotional, motivational, sexual and social behaviour, and memory. Your limbic system determines your emotional style—how you process emotion. More on emotional style in Chapter 2.

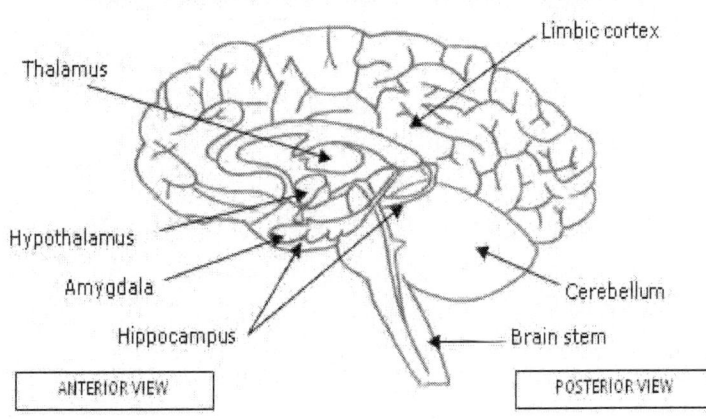

The brain controls all autonomic (involuntary) functions at the same time. These include breathing and heartbeat, as well as the higher mental processes such as thought, and the physical activities of breathing, movement, and coordination, plus non-physical functions such as emotions. It regulates bodily functions and is the seat of your personality. The brain absorbs information (events) from the outside world, interprets it, and makes the body act (respond) accordingly. It does this through a fascinating process of communication between specialised brain or neural cells—called neurons—that fire electrical impulses, or thoughts.

Neurons have tiny branches that reach out and connect to other neurons to form a neuron net. Each place where the neurons connect is integrated into a thought, memory or concept. All concepts in the brain have a possible relationship with one another. The largest web of neocortical functioning in the brain is between the prefrontal cortex area—which regulates emotions—and the limbic structures—which drive emotional impulses; what we call the **emotional brain1**.

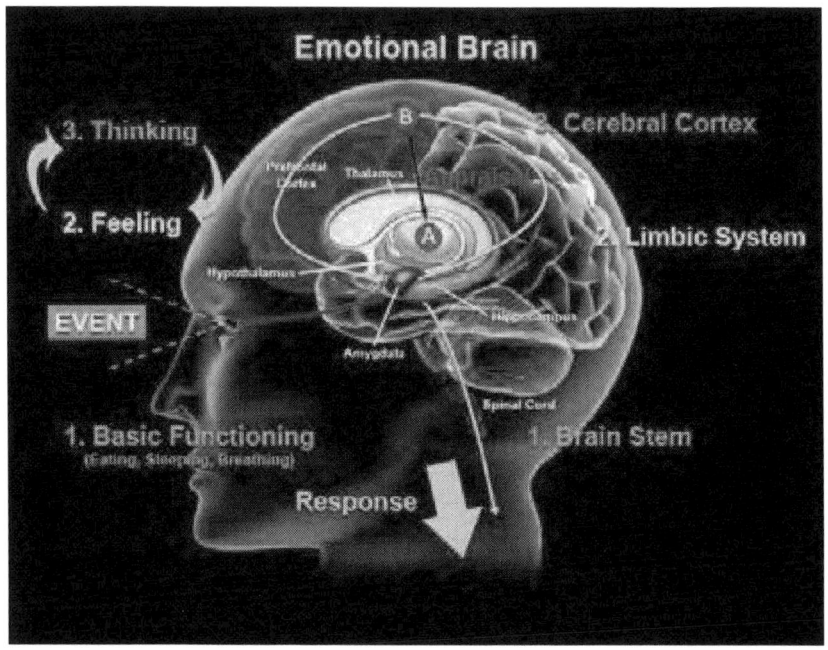

The amygdala is the fear centre of the emotional brain and plays a large role in emotion processing. This perhaps explains the great variety of emotions that humans experience. When you experience an event and a responding impulse—the fight or flight response (the common term for the stress response)— it comes from the amygdala. Once the amygdala is aroused, meaning is then formed through **appraisal** in the frontal cortex—with interaction from the thalamus, hypothalamus, and memory system of the brain—which triggers the emotional response (anger or fear) felt in your body. As the emotional response is mediated by the autonomic nervous system, appraisal is a source of autonomic (involuntary) arousal.

The prefrontal cortex gives the bad feeling we experience in our body a label, and that's the name we give to that emotion. For example, your fi experience on a roller coaster may be exhilarating or terrifying. The memory will be stored as such, and will be recalled as a conditioned response whenever roller coasters are mentioned. Similarly, if you have been chased by a bull in a field, you will have the conditioned response of extreme alertness or fear—a high adrenalin state—when walking in fields. More problematically, if you have been the victim of a betrayal in a marriage, you may remember a feeling of distrust and be overcautious in a future relationship due to that past pain, no matt how trustworthy your new partner may be.

The good news is that cognitive reframing—adjusting your appraisal (perception) of your situation or event in a way that keeps it grounded in the present—allows you to change how you interpret events in the future to have a more meaningful life and increase your joy of living! Before we learn about cognitive reframing, let's take a brief look at the body's autonomic nervous system, the regulatory structure that helps people adapt to changes in their environment.

1.3 Autonomic Nervous System (ANS)

The body's nervous system is comprised of two parts— voluntary and involuntary. We use our **voluntary nerves** to direct our muscles within our body to move, more or less, at will. (It is the central nervous system that we are able to have conscious thought about; for example, movement—blinking and walking.) The autonomic **involuntary nervous system** helps our glands control the functioning of our organs and looks after all the functions over which we have no conscious control. So the autonomic nervous system looks after our heart, lungs, gut and digestion, it looks after our bowels and evacuation, it looks after our reproductive system. These are all the areas of our body that continue to function without us having any conscious control over them.

This involuntary nervous system comprises two subsystems— *sympathetic* and *parasympathetic*. The *sympathetic* nervous sys- tem triggers adrenalin if danger or a threat to the organism is detected. The *parasympathetic* nervous system has a moderating influence; it helps restore balance once the danger or threat has passed.

When our bodies are in a peaceful state, the two branches of the ANS are in check. However, when there is a **stressor (event) or threat** to our person, the *sympathetic* (fight, flight) branch dominates the *parasympathetic* (calming, restorative) branch, and we are aware of our organs functioning. We may feel a racing heart, clammy hands, a tightening in our abdomen, or an urge to use our bowels. *Sympathetic* nerves react this way by means of the chemical adrenalin, which is released at the nerve-endings of the organs concerned. Adrenalin also increases your heart rate, blood pressure and the blood levels of glucose and lipids. We will often hear thrill seekers talk about their adrenalin "pumping".

For any task, there is an optimum level of arousal at which performance will be most efficient. On the whole, moderate levels of arousal seem to act as positive reinforcers and extreme levels of arousal as negative reinforcers. Whether it is stimuli coming to us through our five senses (touch, smell, sound, taste, and sight) from the external world or whether it is our internal thoughts and worries, when we experience a negative emotion (such as anger, fear, sadness, disgust, or surprise) it is our body enduring **the stress response**.

1.4 Stress Felt In the Body

We find it very difficult to manage what we cannot measure. Knowledge is power. So let's look in detail at exactly what is happening to us when we experience the stress response so we can remain in control. We define the effects of stress felt in the body, which arise from nervous arousal, as negative emotion or emotional constipation—commonly referred to simply as 'stress'. The physical effects of accumulated stress felt in the body can be particularly severe.

Not feeling stressed, or feeling positive emotion, is a non- problem status. Your brain interprets that all is right, or right enough, with the world. There is no immediate danger, no threat to your well-being.

However, the moment you feel fear or anger your brain interprets that something is wrong in your environment—there is danger or a threat to your being. "Watch out!" it says. "Be on guard!" This is the fight or flight response in your body. The threat could occur when you are sitting in the dentist's chair, running late for a function, not finding the time to do your tax forms, worrying that your love is unrequited, or learning you have been betrayed. When you feel the perceived threat your body's involuntary (sympathetic) nervous system responds with adrenalin.

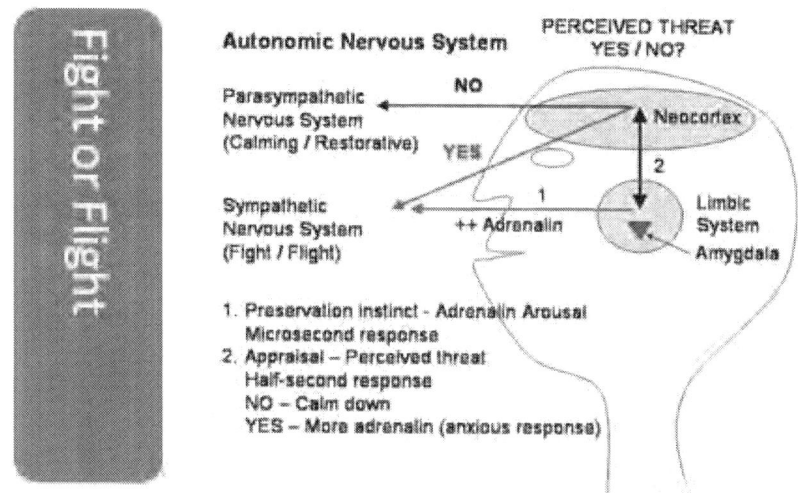

The body manages well with an optimal level of stress. Adrenalin generated to the optimal level of stress is needed for alertness and clarity and for being on guard. The fight or flight response is to do with how your brain deals with managing stress—how you reduce stress after an emotional event.

We considered the two main components of the brain, the limbic system and the cortex. The limbic system, which is deep within the brain, is responsible for the feelings that you have. The cortex is responsible for the thinking.

It is the limbic system, with your fear centre, the amygdala, that will kick off a stress response when your brain interprets that you are under threat—fight or flight. Then the messages go up to the cortex for you to determine, "Is this situation dangerous? Yes or No?". This is illustrated in the diagram to the right.

When your brain recognizes that there is no threat, your *parasympathetic* nervous system puts on the brakes. It stops the flooding of adrenalin and restores your body to calm, so the negative emotion very quickly dissipates.

If your brain interprets, "Yes, there is threat and I am in a dangerous situation and this person is out to attack me," the messages get sent more rapidly down to the *sympathetic* nervous system and more and more adrenalin is produced. Thus, your levels of adrenalin are elevated and this causes you to move into protection mode.

The way we protect ourselves is very much dependent on whether our natural emotional style is more as a 'fight person' or a 'flight person' (Chapter 2).

For example, when your thoughts focus on pain perceived in the future—perhaps due to the possibility of losing your job or partner—your interpretation of this as a threat to your well being will cause your *sympathetic* nervous system to immediately generate adrenalin as the fight/flight response kicks in. The resulting ongoing negative emotions of fear and anxiety could increase your stress beyond the optimal level.

That is, the body produces adrenalin in excess of what the body needs.

Similarly, thoughts focused on memory of pain in the past— such as a betrayal or physical abuse—will increase stress beyond the optimal level.

Higher levels of adrenalin in the body from increased stress will affect the body's ability to cope physically and psychologically. The chemicals adrenalin and noradrenalin that are released by the body's involuntary (sympathetic) nervous system will cause spikes in your adrenalin levels, represented in the diagram below.

Normal Stress

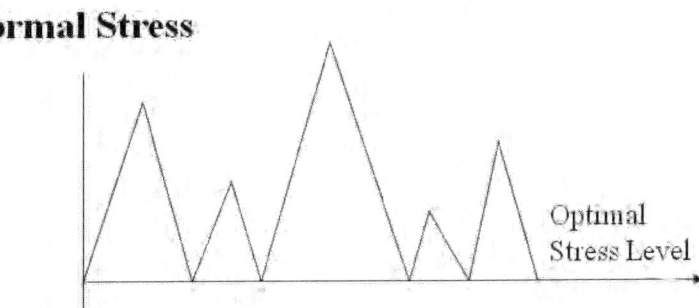

Accumulated adrenalin (stress) can keep you in a heightened state of nervous arousal for some time and will take time for it to be eliminated from the body. Over time, and as the threat to your well being dissipates, the *parasympathetic* nervous system—the calming and restorative arm of the autonomic nervous system—will restore your body to a state of equilibrium or optimal stress level.

Adrenalin arouses your entire nervous system. The emotions aren't allowed to pass as long as you are aroused in this way, so stress accumulates as emotional constipation. Adrenalin stores in the muscles, preparing the body for fight or flight if necessary and only releases once the brain interprets that the threat is over. Unless you can calm yourself down through relaxation, cognitive reframing, meditation, or exercise, the accumulated adrenalin will stay in your body and lead to further adrenalin arousal, possibly trauma, as depicted in the diagram below.

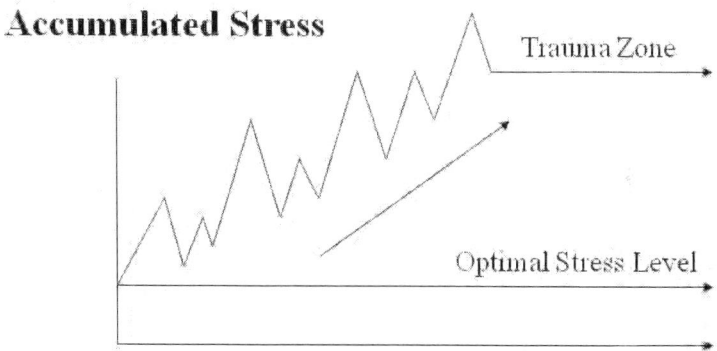

Even when you can recognize that the need for adrenalin has passed, the chemicals will take time to be eliminated from your body. You may continue to shake for a while after the danger has passed, like the zebra.

Every negative emotion you feel is in fact an adrenalin arousal, resulting from your brain assessing that there is some form of threat from your internal or external environment. The experience can be awful, but that is in fact the point. The sole purpose of the stress response is to keep you alert and safe. The more you hate the experience, the more likely you are to avoid the same danger in the future. It is imperative that you listen to your body—and the signals it is giving you. The whole process is your body trying to protect you, not harm you.

It's worth repeating here that when adrenalin remains in the body for an extended period of time, more profound physiological (physical) and psychological (mental) changes occur than just the ability to fight or flee. It can be very helpful to look at some examples of what stress looks like to ensure you are best equipped to avoid it and enjoy emotional health.

1.5 What Stress Looks Like

We have learned that as the adrenalin in our body rises—as we start to accumulate stress—our body experiences ever- increasing physiological reactions. The physiology relates to our physical responses.

- **Example 1**

    A man might come to us and say, "I feel stressed. I feel stressed because of my stressful job." This is interesting because we might say to that man, "Tell us about your job."

    He replies, "Well, I really like my job. I enjoy the people I work with, I'm well paid and I've got a good position." If the man says that to us, we say to him, "Well, you've got a lot of positive feelings about your job. What are the negative feelings? If you don't have any negative feelings then you are actually not stressed. You only experience stress when you have negative emotion. Positive emotion is a non-problem status."

He'll reply, "Well, I'm busy." We'll say, "Well, okay. People who are busy—that's a particular feeling—you can recognize when you are busy, but 'busy' comes and goes. It fluctuates. A negative emotion that you have in your life, the stress that you have in your life, perhaps comes from another source."

Very often, we will explore with that person where his source of stress comes from. It may be related to health. It may be related to low self-esteem. It may be related to his relationship. It may be related to guilt that he has about not spending enough time with his children. But stress is <u>always</u> related to a negative emotion.

- **Example 2**

A house-wife at home says she's stressed and that may be true. She may be feeling bored, lonely, inadequate, helpless, overwhelmed or under-stimulated. Or she may feel put down or dismissed if she tries to tell her husband about these feelings and he says, "What have you got to worry about?"

That sort of comment is likely to make her have even more bad feelings and it therefore increases her stress. Remember, stress is related to a negative emotion and so, yes, we have all sorts of people feeling stressed in all sorts of situations.

Stress is extremely subjective. It relates to how *you* experience it. The stress that we are focusing on in this book is the stress that we experience in any life drama—that could mean a lot of stress. We are referring to a body that is experiencing a lot of stress that can come about through two different ways. It can come about because of one particular life event that causes your body to flood with Adrenalin, for example, a car accident or a tsunami. Or you can also experience a life drama because of 'relentless stress'—an accumulation of stress that occurs over time. In this scenario, there is no particular major event, just a gradual build up of stress through episodes that occur, or negative emotion that you experience, relentlessly— perhaps in your job or your relationship.

If you have a build up of negative emotion and it goes on for a period of time without a break, then you will also become stressed and the feeling is the same. Stress is to do with an accumulation of adrenalin and then a flooding of adrenalin in your body.

- **Case Study—Another Presentation!**

    Situation: Joe came to counseling to try to understand why he experienced so much anxiety about giving presentations at work. The more time he had to prepare, the worse it got. When Joe was asked spontaneously to provide information at a meeting or requested to make a speech on the spur of the moment, he was fine. He said he rather enjoyed those talks, as he could think quickly on his feet, was quite witty, and made people laugh. So why then did he get so worked up when he had to prepare a presentation, even about a subject he knew well?

    Susan's Assessment: Joe was intelligent and confident, and enjoyed the respect and approval of others. When he had time to prepare a presentation weeks in advance, he dwelt on the things he may do incorrectly or go wrong, like omitting important information or having an anxiety attack in front of the audience, and he would experience stress in his stomach just thinking about it. His body was feeling anxiety - anticipation of a negative emotion in the future, and began to produce the stress chemical, adrenalin.

    Work Done In Counseling: I explained to Joe that he was not having anxiety about giving the presentation, but was fearful of experiencing anxiety during the presentation. He had a fear of the fear, which is a phobia. I urged Joe to stay in the present tense as he prepared for his presentation. When he felt his stress level rising, he should concentrate on his body sensations, recognising them as the adrenalin build up in his body. By focusing his thoughts in the present Joe could stop his mind thinking future thoughts, which is enough for the body to begin to discharge some of the adrenalin build up.

Outcome: By keeping his thoughts in the present, Joe learned how to settle his anxious feelings at will.

Susan's Advice For Moving Forward: When we anticipate having fear of something it will cause us stress - negative emotion felt in the body. The more we think about having the anxiety, the worse it gets - because our body is producing more and more of the stress chemical (adrenalin). When we do something spontaneously, there is no time to anticipate things going wrong. If something did go wrong, we would be quick enough and spontaneous enough to cover up or laugh about it, with no build up of stress. Most of us handle things well in the present tense! Adrenalin eases out of the body when there is no more fear or anticipation of fear. Keep your thoughts in the present tense to sett anxious feelings.

1.6 Symptoms of Stress

When you have an extreme level of adrenalin in your body, whether it is caused by one event or whether it is the accumulation of events, your muscles become tighter and tighter and this eventually results in you having physiological responses. Heart palpitations, the chest, neck and shoulders are always involved—you end up feeling quite hunched and very tight around your neck and shoulders.

Whenever you are experiencing stress, one of the common symptoms is muscle ache, especially in the thighs, arms. Your body becomes fatigued because your muscles ache. It is like you have been carrying heavy shopping for a long time and you can't put it down. Even after you have put the heavy shopping down, your muscles still ache because they have been working and tightened for a very long time.

Your breathing is affected. The reason that your breathing alters is simply because your chest wall is a huge muscle. As your muscles constrict and become tighter, the chest wall becomes like a tight, rigid sheet of muscle. As a result of this, the lungs that are inside this chest wall no longer have the ability to expand like they normally do—they are only expanding a little bit and are therefore not taking in the quantity of air that you would normally take in.

After a while the brain sends a signal down to the lungs, "This body needs a little bit more oxygen. Please breathe a bit more deeply." Outwardly, you end up sighing. This forces your chest wall to open to a greater expansion and that is what the (sighing) response is. When you are stressed, you tend to sigh more or you yawn more because yawning has the same impact. Yawning is when you take in air and deliberately force your chest wall to expand. Again, these are symptoms of stress.

Other people will notice that they do not sleep well when they are stressed. Of course not—when you are stressed, your body has got a lot of adrenalin in it. The purpose of adrenalin is to keep you alert, to keep you awake, and to keep you on guard. You are not supposed to sleep when you are on guard duty and so, when you are stressed, you will not be able to sett and you will not be able to sleep because your brain is thinking and checking, "Where is the danger?"

As your stress increases, you are producing more and more adrenalin. The adrenalin that you are producing is making your brain think more and more, "Where is the danger?" A good analogy of this is the meerkat on sentry duty. It is constantly looking around, checking for danger. This is how the brain becomes. It thinks, "Where is the danger?" And so the adrenalin that is genuinely in your body is causing your brain to become more alert, more on guard, worrying. That is why sensitive people, who always have a lot of adrenalin in their body, tend to be worriers. The adrenalin in their body is making their brain think, "Where is the danger?" And then of course, the brain begins to think, "Well, it could be this. It could be that." You are picturing what the danger might be and your body is thereby producing more adrenalin.

This situation becomes the anxious cycle, which when continued, eventually will cause your *parasympathetic* nervous system to break down. The parasympathetic nervous system becomes so exhausted by trying to restore your body to calm that it no longer functions. Now when you are thinking about worrying thoughts your body is producing adrenalin even when you are trying to restore yourself to calm and you are trying to tell yourself, "No, no, no, there is no danger. It's okay. Settle down. You'll get through this. You are a big girl. Other people have experienced things like this before." This is the way we talk to yourself. This is your self-soothing talk.

However, when your *parasympathetic* nervous system breaks down, even as you are trying to calm yourself down, you end up producing more and more adrenalin and this is when you have relentless stress and you can no longer restore to calm. That is when you really experience the feeling of being traumatized.

We are using the word 'trauma' because that is how you feel when you are experiencing a life drama. You feel traumatized. Your body is flooding with adrenalin and it actually feels as though you are in a car accident but the car is still rolling. You don't know what the outcome is going to be. That is how it can feel when you are traumatized.

In the table below we list the most common physical, cognitive, and emotional signs of a stress or trauma reaction.

21

PHYSICAL	COGNITIVE	EMOTIONAL
Nausea, poor appetite	Slowed thinking	Anxiety, Fear
Upset stomach	Difficulty in making decisions	Guilt, Grief
Flatus (gas), Diarrhoea	Difficulty in problem solving	Depression
Profuse sweating	Confusion	Feeling lost
Tremors (lips, hands)	Disorientation (especially to place and time)	Feeling abandoned
Feeling uncoordinated	Difficulty calculating	Feeling isolated
Dizziness	Difficulty concentrating Memory problems	Worrying about others
Chest pain (should be checked at hospital)	Difficulty naming common objects	Wanting to hide
Rapid heartbeat, breathing	Seeing the event over-and-over	Wanting to limit contact with others
Increased blood pressure	Distressing dreams Poor attention span	Anger Irritability
Headaches, Muscle aches		Feeling numb
Sleep disturbance		Startled Shocked
Increased frequency of passing urine		

If these symptoms weren't already enough, the body's ability to recover from stress can collapse completely, leaving the stressed person with escalated adrenalin feelings, lowered self esteem, and an inability to restore to calm, even when the perceived threat has clearly passed, even with positive self- talk and therapy.

It is critical therefore to understand the physiological (physical) and psychological effects of stress if you are to help your body heal.

1.7 Physical Effects Of Stress

The physical (physiological) effects on the body from accumulated stress include:

- A breakdown in the immune system
- An interruption to the autonomic nervous system.
- A decrease in the level of serotonin in the brain

Firstly, when you are feeling stressed, even a little bit stressed, what do you start to notice? You begin to have tummy upsets and when you have a lot of stress, these upsets become more pronounced. The first thing that starts to happen as your autonomic nervous system collapses is that you have a breakdown of your immune system. Excess adrenalin causes your immune system to weaken, meaning you are more likely to pick up viruses and infections. Skin problems resurface, and allergies worsen.

Secondly, as the accumulated adrenalin goes on to impact the autonomic nervous system that copes with digestion, bowel irritation and evacuation, reproduction, and recovery from stress, you can suffer gut and bowel problems. These problems may start small, but can intensify into stomach ulcers or irritable bowel syndrome. The reproductive system is also affected, and often makes conception elusive. For example, researchers now know that stress can have as negative an effect on a man's sperm count and sperm health as it can on the female reproductive cycle.

Thirdly, lowered serotonin leaves you feeling flat, despondent, and depressed, leading to lowered self esteem. We will describe lowered self esteem in the next section (Chapter 1.8).

Adrenalin is designed to make you uncomfortable enough to alter something in your environment so that you feel safer and back in control. However, at elevated levels for long stretches of time, adrenalin becomes a toxin. Once the autonomic nervous system shuts down, it is imperative to seek medical help. The physical symptoms of stress must not be ignored or minimized.

We now turn to the psychological effects of stress—lowered self esteem—and the importance of maintaining high levels of serotonin for emotional health.

1.8 Psychological Effects Of Stress

The inability of the brain to restore calm when flooded with adrenalin is largely due to the fact that sustained adrenalin arousal causes serotonin to be reabsorbed in the brain. Serotonin is the chemical thought to be responsible for maintaining mood and smooth thinking. It keeps the synapses firing; it keeps the brain making its wonderful links and associations. Lowered serotonin leaves one feeling flat, despondent, depressed—with a loss of "joie-de-vivre". This depressed mood state often manifests as lethargy: "I can't be bothered."

Because of the role serotonin plays in mental functioning, lowering it leads to impaired and irrational thinking. The electrical impulses required in thought can't jump across neurons, so thoughts don't spark off in new directions. Instead, the thoughts go around in repetitive circles in the area of the brain where they have just come from, which gives the person a recurring thought. This is the condition of constantly dwelling or ruminating on something, unable to move forward.

When you are feeling down, you dwell on things. It is a cycle of anxiety because the thought you are having is a bad thought. Because you are having a bad thought, your body is creating more adrenalin and so that cycle continues. You try to think something through, and find you can't. This makes you more anxious. The more you worry, the more you worry—your brain is increasing your levels of adrenalin in your body.

Lowered levels of serotonin from stress and recurrent impaired thinking cause lowered self-esteem. Self-esteem is a thinking process. As well as feeling bad, you also think badly about yourself. You have continuous thoughts about how bad you are, how useless you are, how pathetic you are or how uninteresting you are. These ongoing thoughts, in turn, create more and more adrenalin.

An easy way to remember the relationship between serotonin and adrenalin is to consider your hands as two platforms. The left hand is the adrenalin hand and the right hand is the serotonin hand. Remember that these platforms move up and down as though they are a counterweight. As adrenalin rises, serotonin drops. And as adrenalin drops, serotonin rises. Effectively, the label, 'self esteem' could also be placed on the right hand. As adrenalin rises, self esteem is lowered due to lowered serotonin. Your serotonin and your self esteem are intimately connected and they are both strongly influenced by the presence of adrenalin.

For example, you might have a good day spending time with friends. When you get home, you are feeling good. Your serotonin is elevated, you are feeling good about yourself and you are feeling good about life. You do not feel stressed at all. The next day, you might be organizing a dinner-party with the same friends. As you are organizing the dinner party, things go a bit wrong and you discover that you haven't put the wine in the fridge, you haven't got enough meat and the potatoes that you wanted to put on the barbeque turn out to be rotten. Your stress rises, your adrenalin levels rise, you are feeling stressed and now your levels of serotonin have depleted. Because of that, you start all the ruminating thoughts of, "Oh, I'm so hopeless. I should have done that before. Why didn't I check? I'm hopeless at organizing barbeques and my friends aren't going to be happy. And they probably won't even turn up anyway. I'm so pathetic." All of these unnecessary, negative thoughts that you have are simply because of the imbalance of the chemicals in your brain.

Our personal stress is so significantly affected by the way that we think. Once we realize this and visualize this we can work out that if we can change the way we think—if we can change the way that we see a situation and change our viewpoint of it—we are going to change the way that we feel. We are responsible for the way that we feel, regardless of what happens to us in life. We can manage our stress levels and we can work out what we are going to do next by altering the way that we feel. If we do not effetely manage our stress this can lead to lowered self esteem and its inevitable consequence—depression.

How we maintain our self esteem and survive depression and/ or nervous suffering is the subject of Chapter 3. Let us turn now to the highly sensitive person, in whom greater levels of adrenalin are experienced, resulting in genuine physical and psychological distress.

1.9 The Highly Sensitive Person (HSP)

Paul says, "Each morning when I awake, I sit on the side of my bed and remind myself that I'm married and that I have work to do today. But more than that, I'm married to an HSP, so I need to be mindful that what I do and say will more likely have a greater impact on Susan than it may have on others."

The highly sensitive person2 has a limbic system that is highly sensitised to threat, and therefore has a body that produces more adrenalin and faster than another person. This results in the HSP commonly having huge adrenalin arousals which in turn affects their feeling and their thinking. Typically, they will be very aware of what is going on around them, and readily pick up on another's tone of voice, or sideways glance. These may well be interpreted as a threat; hence the HSP often "takes things personally".

It is true that the HSP often feels that they are being attacked or criticised, left out or put down, when that is not actually the case. But because perception is reality, the HSP's interpretation of the event is for them, how they experienced it, how it felt to them. The

HSP has a nervous system that is easily aroused and seldom releases adrenalin as one stimulus after another bombards the limbic system, which is working constantly to appraise for threat.

Generally speaking, being called sensitive has a negative connotation and is suggestive of someone being "moody" or "touchy. Sadly, this is often the case, as HSPs withdraw to protect themselves from any "danger". What the HSP may not realize is that much of the arousal comes from the environment being too noisy, or too bright or hot or sandy or windy. Tags on clothing, lumps in food, tight socks or pants, large crowds or lifts that are too small, can all impact on the sensitive person and cause an adrenalin arousal without them even understanding why. So the HSP is dealing with environmental stimuli and relationship stimuli and often find they have to spend time on their own to "calm down" and build up a tolerance to go out again into the world where there will be more of the same!

A person may say, "I am absolutely certain this bad thing is going to happen. I can feel it!" They'll call it intuition. But this is not intuition. This is anxiety. Your body is producing adrenalin in response to the anticipated bad outcome in your brain. You can feel it as if it has happened. Calm down. It hasn't. In fact, danger doesn't give us the adrenalin response at all. Only the perception of danger does. Anxiety management is perception management.

- **Consider this:**

    If you are running late for a meeting, you feel anxious. If you are running late for a meeting but you are not aware of it because your watch has stopped, you are not anxious. It is only the *perception* of danger that causes your body to release adrenalin. The restoration of calm comes when the brain knows the danger is over—when you finally arrive at your meeting.

- **Consider this:**

    During the Asian tsunami of December 26, 2004, people who perceived the imminent catastrophe experienced the massive adrenalin rush designed to save their lives. They ran enormous distances barefoot, carried unusually heavy burdens, climbed trees when they had never before climbed a tree, and if they survived, they felt no pain until it was all over and the adrenalin ebbed away. Those who noticed the physical changes in the environment before the waves began crashing in— the bubbling water, the sudden expanses of exposed sand and flopping fish—but *didn't* perceive them as dangerous didn't feel the limbic system engage, and didn't flee. When the waves crashed in no doubt many finally experienced the rush and the fight response, but it was too late.

It is important not to confuse arousal with fear. We can be over aroused by semiconscious thoughts or low levels of excitement that create no obvious emotion. It is common for the HSP to feel fearful due to the arousing chemicals produced in the body, even when he does not consciously have anything to feel fearful about. This is commonly what HSP's consider an indication of their "craziness". They have feelings that are incongruous with their intellectual or cognitive awareness of the situation.

One general rule is that when we have no control over stimulation, it is more upsetting; especially if we feel we are someone's victim. While the sound of hammering of your partner finally putting up the bookshelves you've been waiting for can be pleasurable, the sound of the workman's jackhammer outside on the road can be downright irritating.

- **The HSP—Putting Up Fences, Putting Out Fires** Thirty years ago, Paul and Susan owned a 76 acre (30 hectare) rolling hills sheep property in the Adelaide Hills, South Australia. It was a beautiful place with two dams and stocked

with around 100 Border Leicester ewes, which lamb
spring. When they bought the property it had no intern.
fencing, so Paul drew up a design for the various paddocks
and they set about putting up the fences.

One Sunday, the two of them worked all day together, putting in fence posts. This involved Susan holding a new post in position as Paul lined it up from afar. Susan would then hold it in place while Paul came back and dug the hole, then the lining up would happen a second time. Then Paul came back and pushed dirt back into the hole, and made the dirt firm around the post in its new position, using a crowbar. Back and forth, lining up, digging, pushing in soil, and ramming the crowbar. Hard, hard work, hour after hour, the two of them working as a team.

Late in the day, after a large corner post had finally been rammed into position, Paul went back to check the work done. And the corner post was out of alignment (according to Paul's eye that demanded perfection). Paul blew up. He shouted and ranted about the post being in the wrong position, and swore at the "stupid bloody thing" and "now we're just going to have to get it out and do it all over again. It's not good enough."

Susan went quiet, and couldn't believe that Paul could be so mean to her, when she had been nothing but patient and cooperative all day. How could he attack her like that?

The tension between them did not abate that evening, and Susan gave Paul the "cold shoulder" into the next day whilst she waited for an apology from him for his unnecessary outburst. An apology did not come, so the "no talking" between them continued. Not a word between them until later on the Tuesday, when civil courtesy returned, "Do you want something to eat?" "Can you drive me to work tomorrow?" But no warmth. Susan was still waiting for an apology. She had been wounded and believed that Paul should apologize for his behaviour on the Sunday.

On Thursday, fed up with the silence, Paul asked Susan, "So when are we going to start speaking again? What are you sulking about?" Susan was incensed. "I'm not sulking. I'm wounded." "What on earth are you wounded about?" Paul wailed, totally frustrated. "What have I done now?"

Sarcastically, Susan said, "You know very well what you've done. I'm wounded because you yelled at me." Bewildered, Paul said, "Yelled at you? When did I yell at you?" And so with great self-righteous indignation, Susan repeated word for word, what Paul had yelled at her on Sunday. She had dwelt on it so many times since then, she now knew the scene off by heart.

Paul was flabbergasted at Susan's disclosure. He protested and said, "But I wasn't yelling at you! I was yelling in frustration because the fence post was crooked. I was the one doing the lining up, so if I was yelling at anyone, I would have been yelling at myself! Whatever made you think I was yelling at YOU?"

Sheepishly now, Susan said, "Well of course I would think you were yelling at me, I was the only one there." Susan of course, being a sensitive and avoidant person, had not ever yelled at a person, and certainly not at an inanimate object. That to her, didn't make sense. No wonder she had assumed that Paul had been yelling at her. But she suddenly realised she had got it wrong, which explained why there had been no apology.

Then Paul asked the question that changed the course of their relationship. He said, "So I wasn't yelling at you but anyway, even if I was, how did that make you feel?" Susan finally was given the opportunity to release what had been going around in her head for four days. "When you yell at me, I feel disrespected, I feel you don't value me, I feel like I'm a nuisance and that you don't want me doing things with you, I feel you don't love me and that you wish you weren't married to me."

Susan could see Paul was flabbergasted as he gasped, "You feel all those things when I yell at you?" "Yes" Susan replied, with the tone that indicated, "Of course, doesn't everyone?"

Paul continued, "Nothing could be further from the truth. I had absolutely no idea you feel that when I yell! Because I do respect you and I do value you. I do not consider you a nuisance and I love doing things with you. I absolutely love you and I always want to be married to you. I cannot believe you think those things because I yell! However, now that I know that that is what you feel, I am going to try very hard not ever to raise my voice again when you are around. But I have always yelled and I am bound to make mistakes. So if my part of the bargain is that I will try not to yell at you, can YOUR part of the bargain please be that when I make a mistake and I do yell, can you please say to yourself, "This does NOT mean he doesn't respect me, this does NOT mean he doesn't value me, this does NOT mean he doesn't love me." Because Susan, those thoughts are only your interpretation. It is not reality."

This event was a turning point for Susan as it was the first time in her life that she realized that not everyone experienced events the same way that she did, and that her interpretation of events and feelings were hers alone. This helped her understand why she had been hurt by people's words and actions in the past, when she had been puzzled that a person would behave in a way so very different to how she would behave. And she also realized she wasn't always right and that she had to be careful about her "holier than thou" attitude at times, which she realized, impacted on others.

Positive Aspects of Being Sensitive

There are many!

- HSP's are better at spotting errors and avoiding making errors—the perfectionist is likely to be an HSP.

- They are able to concentrate deeply (best without distractions), and are highly conscientious.

- They are often thinking about their own thinking but this is not self-centeredness, rather more inner reflections and musings.

- They are able to process material deeply, and are usually analysing something with emotional content about self or others.

- HSP's learn without being aware that they have learned, simply by their being aware of things happening in their environment.

- They make good forensic investigators!

- They are usually very empathic and compassionate people as they are deeply affected by other people's moods and emotions.

- HSP's are usually more "right-brained"—less linear, more creative.

How you act following your perception or interpretation of a threat from your internal or external environment, and whether or not you are an HSP, will depend upon your dominant emotional style. It is to this we now turn in the next chapter.

2
Know Your Emotional Style — How You Deal With Your Emotions

2.1 Introduction

If you experience a balance of good and bad feelings in the course of a day, it is unlikely that you will experience stress. If you experience predominantly bad or negative feelings you will accumulate stress. Recall from Chapter 1 that stress is a build up of negative emotion felt in the body, experienced as nervous arousal—we call this accumulated stress or 'emotional constipation'.

We have explained that too much stress felt in the body produces adrenalin above optimal levels. But why is it that some people experience higher levels of stress than others? This is because there are two **emotional styles**.

People with an *avoidant* emotional style are more prone to retaining stress, as they feel each emotion with a greater intensity and are less likely to deal with it immediately than people with a *reactive* style. Discovering which style you are will give you insight into the emotions centre of your brain, and how to manage your response to an emotional event in a way that will lead to greater emotional well-being.

The way you react to the feeling of stress depends on whether you are more inclined by nature to be a fight (reactive) person or a flight (avoidant) person. We tend to adopt more of a fight or flight personality as a way of dealing with events in our life. Some people store up emotions, some let rip with aggression and passion.

The *reactive* person generally processes his or her emotion immediately, by displaying the emotion—irritation, frustration or anger—or by needing to discuss the matter right away to resolve it. He or she cannot wait, and will even pursue a partner or colleague from room to room to discuss the matter and resolve it, becoming increasingly angry en route. Being angry or upset is how a reactive person is trying to release adrenalin, to stop pain.

Once the reactive person has blurted out their hurt or frustration they will be calmer because their adrenalin levels would have returned to their optimal level. Unfortunately, the result is often more anger. Through its negative impact on others, anger, frustration and loud tones tend to generate more anger rather than resolve it.

If a person is *avoidant*, and particularly if they are also sensitive, anger will frighten him or her, causing emotional withdrawal and termination of communication. Avoidant people are often "pleasers" who above all seek to avoid being disliked, disapproved of, or criticized. They can come across as calm under fire, but this is often merely because they are protecting themselves with the flight response, unable to speak, unable to process what is happening in a rational way until the arousal has passed.

It takes a tremendous amount of energy and effort for the avoidant person to speak up over the adrenalin, and if the situation doesn't change, they will experience more adrenalin arousals.

Conversely, it takes a tremendous amount of energy and effort for the reactive person to keep quiet and not express frustration or anger when aroused.

2.2 Reactive and Avoidant Emotional Styles

Paul and Susan are married. We are both highly educated and intelligent. Paul has an MBA and a PhD in emotional intelligence. Susan holds a BA in social work and a Masters in Public Health. Both of us have been successful in our careers, raised a family, traveled widely, and have offered advice and support to thousands of people from all walks of life and 83 nationalities to improve human wellness. We are stable and influential, in a relationship lasting over 36 years. We have collaborated to provide clients with the benefit of our combined knowledge and experience in life in our books, digital products and membership site.

But we each have a different emotional style. We respond very diff to the same event, and experience emotion in totally different ways. Because we are both fully aware of our emotional style and the physiological impact it has on us and on others, we experience and manage our worlds very diff

Here's how it is for Susan:

"Once I learned how my adrenalin floods affected everything I did, life became much more enjoyable and easier.

I have always gone along with what other people wanted, deferred to their wishes and opinions, in order to manage my adrenalin levels. My happiness came from harmony in my environment, as conflict or even potential conflict resulted in adrenalin floods. If I perceived that a person might judge me, disapprove of me, be disappointed in or feel let down by me, I would feel so dreadful that I would go out of my way ensure that this did not happen. This is my *avoidant* emotional style, my flight response.

Once I've had an adrenalin flood I need to process it out of my body and return to normal. After a conflict it takes me a long time to warm up again. I experience my negative emotions intensely (the burden of the highly sensitive person) and avoid any situation that might cause an escalation of that feeling. I was an obedient teenager (lest my parents be cross with me), a diligent student (lest my teachers think badly of me), helpful to all (lest people consider me selfish and dislike me) and a wife who withdrew and internalized in order to avoid conflict.

I am learning that my avoidant behaviour impacts Paul, who feels punished and excluded. Paul tells me, 'Just because you have an avoidant emotional style doesn't mean that you have a monopoly on negative emotion.' This is something I need to be constantly aware of and recognize when considering the impact of my behaviour on others.

My appreciation of how I deal with my emotions has improved my overall well-being. Managing my avoidant emotional style releases adrenalin from my body, making me emotionally well."

Paul says:

"I learned at great personal cost, with the loss of my first wife and twin daughters nearly 40 years ago, that loud tones, aggression, irritation, and anger had to go.

I have always been a leader, full of ideas and the energy, persistence, and dedication to carry them all out. I used not to suffer fools gladly and felt quickly frustrated, irritated, and angry when things did not go my way. I could explode like a bomb! As a man, I was used to summing up a situation, weighing alternatives, implementing them, and looking for results. I often did all this in my head without too much discussion, not realizing fully that my behavior, including loud tones and quick words, impacted Susan so adversely.

Susan tells me, 'It doesn't matter what you say to me, just say it in a normal voice. When someone speaks to me in an irritable tone, I perceive that you are cross with me for what I just said. That leaves me feeling unfairly judged.' This is what I need constantly to be aware of, as a person who has a *reactive* emotional style, when considering the impact of my behavior on others.

My reactive style—the fight style—means that I deal with events as they happen. I still react to things quite quickly, but I am learning to put a gap between my thoughts and emotions to allow me time, to better manage the negative emotion generated by my reactive style. Now I recognize the negative emotion in my body on a scale from 1 to 10, with 1 being low intensity and 10 being rage. By the time I feel my negativity rising to level five or six, I can usually insert a gap in my response and deal with my dis-ease in an emotionally intelligent way, releasing adrenalin from my body.

As I respond to events, I recognize that only I can make myself irritated, frustrated, and angry. It's not the event. It's me. So I manage my emotional style in a way that elevates my emotional well-being. I feel much healthier. And Susan is happier for it."

In summary;

Paul has a reactive emotional style. You can read about this at length in our book (2004), *Emotional Leadership. Using emotionally intelligent behaviour to enjoy a life of EASE.* Over the last 40 years, following the separation from his first wife and the admonition from Susan; "Paul, it's not what you say, it's the way you say it!", Paul has learned, and continues to learn, to adjust his reactive emotional style—the way he feels and expresses the negative emotions of irritation, frustration and anger. It is, as you will discover, an ongoing process.

Susan has an avoidant emotional style, meaning she feels and holds in predominantly the negative emotions of anxiety, bewilderment and withdrawal, which is also covered in detail in our earlier book. In addition, Susan is a highly sensitive person (HSP) — which means she feels her emotions intensely—and is often experiencing nervous arousal with adrenalin floods, but she has learned to manage it. She feels she is 'in charge'; and she feels settled, which is the state in which she functions best. Through cognitive reframing and a course of medication she can now create that settled state whenever the need arises.

Both Paul and Susan experience positive emotion to a high degree. If you experience a balance of good and bad feelings, it is unlikely that you will accumulate stress. And that has to be good news!

- **Case Study—Diff Styles, Diff Vocabularies Situation:** A couple who came to see Susan for counseling, deep in the throes of misunderstandings and resentments, did her the favor of laying out the very particular vocabularies that match the very different feelings of the two emotional styles. While they were accustomed to talking about how they fought, they hadn't discussed what they *felt* when they fought.

    Susan's Assessment: Susan laid their feelings out on a scale of 1 to 10, with 1 being how they felt at the beginning of the incident and 10 being the feeling at the height of it. We call these anxiety and anger scales. The wife, whose emotional style was *avoidant*, had an anxiety scale list like this:

    10. Rage (High intensity)
    9. Furious
    8. Misrepresented
    7. Attacked
    6. Misunderstood
    5. Criticised
    4. Blamed
    3. Churned up
    2. Uneasy
    1. Queasy (Low intensity)

    Meanwhile, the *reactive* husband's anger scale list looked like this:

    10. Vindictive (High intensity)
    9. Resentful
    8. Pissed off
    7. Irritated
    6. Frustrated
    5. Disrespected
    4. Not valued
    3. Dismissed
    2. Rejected
    1. Unwanted (Low intensity)

Susan's Advice For Moving Forward: If either of these different ways of responding to events in your life is very familiar to you, you have now established which emotional style your amygdala favors, and you can begin to manage it, just as this couple did. Each was quite surprised that the other had not felt the same as them during their fights, and could finally begin to adjust to their marked differences. We can't manage what we can't measure. It's time to begin measuring your emotional style using the anxiety and anger scales listed above and and start managing your emotions.

- **Case Study—The Avoidant Person**

    Situation: Susan explores how and why an avoidant person acts the way they do, and the impact that it has on others.

    Bev and Mark came for counseling, because of a huge family blow-up that had occurred over Christmas when the family had come together. During the dispute, Mark had told their adult kids to "pack up and leave", which they had duly done, and now no longer had contact with them. Bev was distressed over the lack of contact with the children and grandchildren, and was blaming Mark for the family split.

    Mark said that, not for the first time, his wife "sided" with the children when they argued with and disrespected him, and this left him feeling the "bad guy" in the argument. Mark said that he constantly felt unsupported by his wife, and that this was the reason he had completely 'blown up' on this occasion. He said that her lack of support really hurt him.

    Work Done Counseling: In counseling, Bev had a chance to speak without fearing Mark's anger. She said that she felt sick whenever there was a hint of conflict and that over the years she had acted as peacemaker, so as to minimise situations when Mark might flare up. She hated the arguments more than anything, and would agree with the children so they would settle down and not argue with their father. Time and time again she would say to Mark, "It's not what you say, it's how you say it". It was only in counseling that Mark realized that it was his anger and loud tones that was having the impact on Bev, not the content of the disagreement. Many times Bev actually agreed with him (e.g., that the son needed discipline or the daughter was out of line) but her wish to minimise conflict was being interpreted by him as her being "against" him.

Outcome: Susan explained to Mark that whilst he felt unsupported by her, his wife felt embarrassed, anxious, humiliated, and scared every time he raised his voice or got angry. This resulted in her withdrawal from him, in communication, affection and support.

Susan's Advice For Moving Forward: The avoidant person needs to release their resentments by expressing how they feel, however if there is any risk of further outbursts or conflict, their fear will result in them saying nothing, and the feeling of resentment and disgust escalates.

It is important to know that these emotional styles are not gender specific. A male person can be avoidant or reactive and vice versa. Until these styles are understood, appreciated, and adapted to suit the needs of the relationship, there will be ongoing emotional and physical pain. The good news is that knowing and understanding your emotional style means you can stop blaming someone else for the way you feel!

2.3 Who's to blame?

A good way you can think of these styles is in terms of volcanoes! On the one hand, the *avoidant* style has a larger volcano. The avoidant person is slow to anger. His or her hurts build up over time.

Just because he or she doesn't bring them up as an issue doesn't mean they don't exist. (It also doesn't mean that her partner, friend, or boss should know they are there.) When the pent up hurts eventually grow so numerous that they put too much pressure on his or her volcano, he or she may not get angry, but may withdraw completely from engagement in the relationship. But when an avoidant person's volcano does blow, you want to be well clear as it is very intense heat!

On the other hand, the *reactive* person's volcano is small. Fewer threats are necessary for an explosion to occur. Sometimes this person reacts to adrenalin faster and will go ahead and display the emotion. This is his or her way of de-stressing. If his partner is avoidant, however, it is likely to lead to future stress, because her subsequent withdrawal can seem like neglect to him or, as in the case study above, lack of support.

The hardest thing to grasp, when we aren't aware of our emotional style and its role in our behavior, is the problem of blaming another for the way we feel. We say things like, "You are making me feel like X," or "You always make me feel so Y." People say things like this to others all the time. We say it to our friends: "She makes me feel so stupid." And our friends nod and say, "I know." We think that if we feel bad because of someone's behavior, we can't feel good until they change *their* behaviour. But as Eleanor Roosevelt pointed out, "No one can make you feel inferior without your consent."

It is imperative that Susan acknowledge that the only person who can make Susan anxious, is Susan. Susan is responsible for how she feels— No one else! However, Paul can be mindful of Susan's emotional style and not say or do things that will raise her level of arousal.

If we can change our perspective of the threat, we can change how we feel. For example, when Paul reacts with frustration or irritation in any given situation, Susan no longer takes it so personally. She puts the necessary gap between the event and her reaction to it—she takes time to analyse the threat—to remember that this is his way of de-stressing. She can now say to herself, "I'm not scared of this. I know what this feeling is." She reminds Paul that if he needs to talk to her about it, he needs to do so in a calm tone so that she doesn't withdraw. And this reminds Paul of his emotional style as well. She will still get upset, but not nearly as upset as she used to be. We measure it, we manage it, and above all, we maintain our bond using a sound survival strategy.

2.4 Surviving Your Emotional Style

Understanding and taking responsibility for your emotional style is an extremely important strategy to survive your life dramas. And there are many other related strategies that can add up to a life of ease. We need to look at ways to naturally elevate serotonin; good feeling activities. Here is a list that can help both avoidant and reactive types:

1. Understand the two levels of fear: limbic fear, which comes without language, and the cognition/thought that follows, which is expressed to the self in words. This is cognitive awareness. Remember that level two thoughts are to do with the future, and that the future isn't reality. Stay in the present.

2. In order to manage staying in the present and calming your fears in the current reality, think about your body. Observe your physical reaction to the situation and talk yourself through it rather than being controlled by it. Learn and apply the 4-step cognitive framework (Chapter 3.10).

3. Meditation and yoga are excellent strategies for managing your body and your mind. They both encourage a release from emotional constipation, so that thoughts can be experienced without fear.

4. When aroused, practise breathing out for longer than you breathe in. The concentration this requires will calm your

brain, and the slow breathing will calm your heart. Your brain will interpret this as a return to your normal state, and will stop sending adrenalin through your body.

5. Smile. Even a fake smile will send chemicals to the brain that will trick it into thinking you feel better. Again, adrenalin production will decline. This is very effective.

6. Sing along to music. Loud! Singing allows for both emotional and physical release. Once you've sung your heart out, you can return to the question at hand with a clearer brain.

7. Exercise is a similarly powerful strategy, as it uses up stored adrenalin and increases serotonin production in the brain. Even if you feel too exhausted by anxiety to exercise... exercise anyway.

- **Case Study— Unexpected Behavior**

    Susan describes a situation, which brought unexpected behavior. She was working as a social worker in the trauma room of the local hospital. She sat with a married couple whilst they waited for information about their teenage daughter who had been involved in a car smash and brought into the trauma room by ambulance. Susan had had the unpleasant task of ringing each parent at work and asking them to come into the hospital, as their daughter had undergone emergency surgery for her life threatening injuries.

    When the doctor finally arrived, his solemn attitude gave a moment's preparation of the news that he brought. Sadly, he told the parents, their daughter had not survived surgery and had died due to major head trauma sustained in the accident. On hearing the news, the father became immobilized and withdrawn in shock. He said nothing, nor did he display any emotion of distress. He simply looked stunned—a frozen, "deer in the headlights" reaction. He did not reach out to support his wife, which may have been his shock reaction or an indication that the two were not very connected, and he was processing his emotions alone.

The mother had a reaction seldom seen but also "normal" in a trauma situation. The mother burst into laughter. The doctor, puzzled, told her that he was not joking, and that what he was telling her was for real. The mother kept laughing and Susan quietly explained to the doctor that laughter can be a shock reaction. Laughter and distress are emotions that are closely aligned, even though they seem to be contradictory emotions. After all, we laugh until we cry. We also sometimes cry until we laugh, do we not?

The mother was deeply distressed and her laughter quickly turned into uncontrollable sobbing. She struggled to understand her reaction, and felt guilty at having laughed at such dreadful news. Susan was able to console her and explain that at times of trauma, any reaction can be considered "normal", as the brain is processing the threat and what it means to the person. While this processing is going on, a person's reaction will also depend on whether they have a predominantly "reactive" or "avoidant" response to perceived danger.

In the next chapter we talk about how we generate emotion and what is meant by putting a 'gap' between an event and our response to it. We call this EAR-Identity, which arises from self-interaction. Once understood, EAR-Identity and the 4-step cognitive framework will enable you to eliminate the causes of emotional stress and create the life of your dreams.

3

Understand How You Generate Emotion
—
Get Smart At Noticing your Emotions

3.1 Introduction

Emotions represent bodily feelings that you experience as nervous arousal—an arousal of the nervous system. No one else can experience your feelings in the same way that you do. An implication of this fact is that you have to be responsible for your feelings. They're not happening to anyone else. Emotion states represent affective experience—they are generated to signal a need. But how are states of emotion generated? Can emotions be controlled?

Emotion states are brought forth both biologically and consciously, in response to an event. Emotions are brought forth *biologically* when bodily feelings of hunger and lack of sleep, or allergic reaction to certain food substances such as gluten and wheat, act as stimuli to change one's internal chemistry. Emotions are brought forth *consciously* in the drama of life.

You are what you think. You create your mood and emotional style. You are responsible for your behavior. Only *you* can make you angry or anxious. You *can* change the way you think and your behavior. You can choose to own your feelings and take responsibility for them. Or you can choose to be a victim. This is well illustrated by the following quote (accurate source unknown).

Watch your thoughts for they become words. Watch your words for they become actions. Watch your actions for they become habits. Watch your habits, for they become your character. And watch your character, for it becomes your destiny!

Emotions are expressions of awareness, the fundamental stuff of life. Being aware, you participate in every reaction that takes place inside you. But you are not stuck in your life cycle. The problems arise when you don't take responsibility for what you're doing.

The contemporary view is that emotions convey information about relationships. Each emotion signals a different relation. And each of us experiences our emotion differently. Thoroughly thinking through and understanding our emotions and the emotions of others is an important source of coping—with ourselves, friends, family, workmates, and community—and solving behavioral problems.

3.2 Label Emotions

With the development of language, the sensations we experience were given names or labels; such as, anger, fear, disgust, sadness, surprise and enjoyment. These labels allow us to communicate to others how we feel. Because our perceptions or subjective experiences are diff there is no uniformity of terminology used to describe emotions. Therefore the terms affect, feelings, and emotions are used interchangeably. Some definitions;

Affective states: Denominates, generically, events experienced as feelings or emotions.

Feelings: Affective states that have a longer duration— causing less intensive experiences—with fewer physiological repercussions on the body, and lowered interference on reasoning and behaviour. For example; impatient, startled or bored.

Emotions: An emotion is a feeling with a thought. From the Latin "emovere"—meaning moving, displaces. Emotions are manifest reactions to affective conditions that—due to their intensity—move us to some kind of action, response or behavior. Emotions are characterised by a disruption of affective balance, and can have long-term physical and physiological effects on the body, as discussed in Chapter 1.

Positive or negative energy states: A person will experience both positive emotions (pleasure) and negative emotions (pain) throughout their life. These two energy states have a strong impact on emotional health. We can think of positive emotions as adding energy (energising) and negative emotions as subtracting energy (draining).

Paul Ekman3 (1992) has given us generic group labels for basic emotions or emotion families.

3.3 Six Emotion Families

Figure 3.1—Emotions classified according to intensity.

ANGER	FEAR	SADNESS	ENJOYMEN	DISGUST	SURPRISE
High Intensity Emotions					
betrayed	desperate	crushed	alive	abused	aghast
controlled	distrustful	dejected	confident	appalled	bewildered
criticised	insecure	disillusioned	determined	betrayed	confounded
deceived	isolated	distraught	energetic	coerced	distracted
furious	intimidated	fragile	excited	humiliated	flabbergasted
hostile	panic-stricken	insecure	indestructible	rejected	flustered
misunderstood	scared	unable to cope	overjoyed	shamed	misinterpreted
outraged	terrified	unloved	powerful	trapped	perplexed
resentful	terrorised	unwanted	secure	used	shocked
revengeful	threatened	vulnerable	trusting	violated	stunned
Medium Intensity Emotions					
angry	agitated	alone	accepted	awkward	amazed
attacked	anxious	deflated	capable	burdened	disoriented
bitter	claustrophobic	depressed	content	disrespected	embarrassed
defensive	fearful	discouraged	full of life	guilty	horrified
embarrassed	frightened	drained	happy	jealous	puzzled
excluded	harassed	miserable	healthy	overwhelmed	startled
frustrated	panicky	pathetic	loving	punished	taken aback
indignant	pressured	run down	positive	suspicious	unprepared
irritated	tense	unhappy	relaxed	unloved	unsettled

| ANGER | FEAR | SADNESS | ENJOYMEN | DISGUST | SURPRISE |

Low Intensity Emotions

ANGER	FEAR	SADNESS	ENJOYMEN	DISGUST	SURPRISE
annoyed	afraid	despondent	aglow	disapproved of	astonished
bothered	alarmed	disappointed	bright	distrustful	baffled
cross	concerned	disbelief	bubbly	inferior	bothered
disgruntled	lonely	dismayed	calm	insecure	dazed
distracted	nauseous	down	glad	offended	disappointed
disturbed	shaky	lethargic	good	self-conscious	disconcerted
fed up	unsure	low	joyful	self-righteous	disorganised
troubled	uptight	solemn	light-hearted	unattractive	mixed up
upset	worried	useless	smiling	unimportant	uncertain

Each emotion family is a grouping of related states or variations.

Many researchers recognize the minimum for cognitive activated emotion as appraisal. Your appraisal mechanism operates rapidly, but is not always automatic—as when there is a slow, deliberate and conscious evaluation of the event that triggered the emotion state. Automatic appraisal does not simply and solely operate on what is given biologically— dealing only with stimulus events that exactly fit what is given. Individual differences in our experience allow for enormous variations in the specifics of what calls forth emotion that are attributable to personality, family, and culture. We will develop our understanding of the appraisal mechanism in the next section (Chapter 3.4), titled: EAR—Identity.

3.4 EAR—Identity: The Person You Want To Be

To begin a cognitive-behavioural explanation of the role emotions play in your well-being, you need explore your "trigger", the source of arousal, using the **EAR—Identity** framework.

EAR—Identity

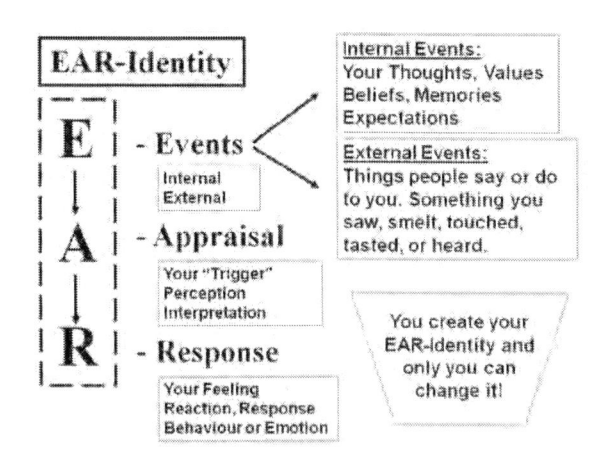

- **E** – Events
  - Internal
  - External
- **A** – Appraisal
  - Your "Trigger"
  - Perception
  - Interpretation
- **R** – Response
  - Your Feeling Reaction, Response Behaviour or Emotion

Internal Events: Your Thoughts, Values Beliefs, Memories Expectations

External Events: Things people say or do to you. Something you saw, smelt, touched, tasted, or heard.

You create your EAR-Identity and only you can change it!

EAR—Identity is the identity that you have created for yourself—the person you want to be. It arises from self-interaction. It is how you manage your response after an emotional event. The diagram opposite depicts your response generated by your appraisal of an internal event (thought, value, belief, memory, expectation) or external event (from your senses) mediated by the amygdala—thalamus—cortex interaction in your brain (Chapter 1.)

When your EAR—Identity consistently responds with right behavior, neither as reactive nor avoidant, but a good balance of the two, people will develop trust in you and approach you as someone who is approachable, predictable and a mentor.

In Chapter 2 we discussed the two emotional styles—avoidant and reactive. We explained how when you react spontaneously to an event with a negative emotion, you will either display anger, irritation and frustration (reactive/fight) or anxiety, bewilderment and withdrawal (avoidant/flight). Neither reaction enhances a relationship if managed badly.

EAR—Identity helps you develop and use impulse control by putting a 'gap' between the event and your response to it. In doing so, you will have learned to better manage your response to an emotional event.

Give yourself a chance to see the event from a different perspective and the chance to consider how you will respond— whether you will say something, what you will say, how you will say it and the tone of voice you will use. Altering your appraisal of events will change your mind, change your life. EAR—Identity shows you how.

Stress is a result of your appraisal of an event. Sometimes your appraisal is correct. Sometimes it is not.

- Example 1:
  <u>Event</u>: There is an earthquake. <u>Correct Appraisal</u>: I'm in danger. <u>Response</u>: Stress.

- Example 2:
  <u>Event</u>: A husband raises his voice in an angry tone.
  <u>Incorrect Appraisal by wife</u>: He's mad at me.
  <u>Response</u>: Stress.

EAR—Identity is your strategy to always be the person you want to be; to always behave the way you want to behave. To be predictable and consistent with each response to each event, so as not give away your power. And to retain responsibility for your response.

You cannot then say to someone, "You made me do this", "You made me feel this", or "See what you did to me". Others will be able to predict or anticipate a consistent response from you whenever they approach you to talk. They may not get agreement but they will get kindness, honesty, non- judgment and a listening ear, rather than sometimes getting kindness, sometimes being dismissed, sometimes experiencing irritability, or being put-down.

Using EAR—Identity your response now becomes your new conscious response, replacing a former negative pre- conditioned auto-response. After a period of time and practise, your conscious response will in itself become a conditioned positive auto-response, displaying the behavior you want to be. As a consequence, EAR—Identity allows you to feel in control of your behavior; able to put a GAP between your events and responses.

3.5 Use The Gap To Give My Life Meaning

The key to both your emotional growth and happiness is how you use the Gap between event and response—how you appraise events and give meaning to each event in your life.

It is in the Gap that your appraisal of events impacts the amount of adrenalin your body has to deal with and eventually expel to restore balance to your emotional state of arousal.

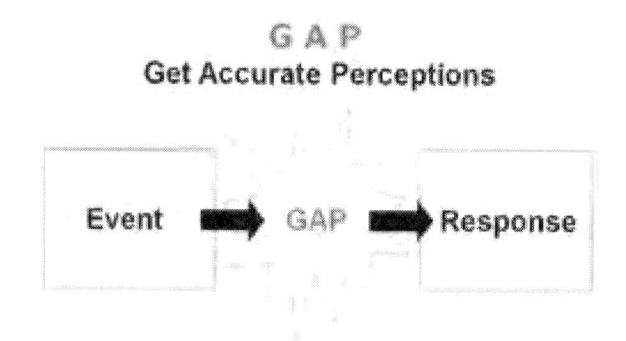

G A P
Get Accurate Perceptions

Event ➡ GAP ➡ Response

It is in the GAP that you have the Power
to choose behavior you want to be!

It is in the Gap that you have the power to reframe your EAR—Identity.

Central to EAR—Identity is appraisal—your perception of how you know the world. Knowing yourself, the world, and understanding change, is to recognise that it is your perception or interpretation (appraisal) of events that causes emotional constipation and behavioral problems—not the events themselves.

Our assumptions are (1) the event (internal or external information) precedes response (behaviour), and (2) emotion is thought plus feeling—where thought precedes feeling. These assumptions are necessary in order to understand how you are able to change your appraisal of an event—the "trigger" for your response—using a 4-step process.

In Chapter 1.8, The Psychological Effects of Stress, we wrote about lowered self esteem and the importance of maintaining high levels of serotonin for emotional health. Negative appraisal—the human capacity for judgement—leads to lowered self esteem through the repetitive negative messages of the inner voice, whose goal is to disrupt your capacity to form an EAR—Identity that will overcome emotional constipation caused by adrenalin arousal. If you are behaving the way you want to behave you will feel proud. If you are not behaving the way you want to behave you will be beating yourself up and thinking how terrible you are. To help you be the person you want to be we provide a 4-step cognitive framework (Chapter 3.10). But before we visit the 4-step process, let's explore our understanding of self esteem and how we can control the inner voice—that voice in your head that keeps telling you that you are no good.

3.6 Understand Self Esteem

Self-esteem is your inner view of yourself. Others may give you other-esteem, that is, they like and respect you, but you can have low self-esteem nonetheless if your inner view of yourself is of a person not good or not worthy—that is, you reject yourself.

A person may feel a fraud, and worry that others may not like him if they knew what he was REALLY like.

As the first three levels of your needs (physiological needs; safety and security; affection and belonging) are met, you will look for a little esteem from others. You do not begin to have a need for the esteem of others unless, and until, you first feel safe and loved. Receiving love from your parents, family and friends ensures that your inner view of self—your self- esteem—has a solid grounding. But without self-esteem you won't necessarily feel loved.

In describing the nature of self-esteem, Mackay and Fanning (2000, p. 1)[4] write;

One of the main factors differentiating humans from other animals is the awareness of self—the ability to form an identity and then attach a value to it. In other words, you have the capacity to define who you are, and then decide if you like that identity or not. The problem of self-esteem is this human capacity for judgment. It's one thing to dislike certain colors, noises, shapes, or sensations. But when you reject parts of yourself, you greatly damage the psychological structures that literally keep you alive.

Self-esteem is a thought process that translates to a feeling. If you do not translate the negative feeling back to a thought you will not be able to challenge the message. For example, you feel uncomfortable when you enter a room of unknown people at a cocktail function. The feeling (adrenalin arousal) is of discomfort or nervousness or anxiety. What is the internal message? It can readily be translated to:

- "I do not belong here", or
- "I am not suitably dressed, and people will notice" or
- "No-one is going to want to talk to me" – or similar.

Once you catch the message and challenge it, you can see that the message is inaccurate or irrational, or at best, completely exaggerated. If you can cognitively talk down the irrational message (with positive self-talk or using the 4-step process) then you will reduce the negative emotion and feel confident enough to go up to a stranger and introduce yourself. You are, after all, as unique as the next person and have just as much right to be at this function as him.

In our view, it is better to speak of lowered rather than low self-esteem, as a person's self-esteem fluctuates with every situation. Rarely does a person have consistent bad feelings about himself. The inner view fluctuates with the fluctuations of chemicals and negative feelings inside him. You can feel fine and completely capable at one time of the day (for example, about being an organized working mum) and later in the same day feel dreadful that you are a neglectful and completely irresponsible parent.

For example, you may feel like an irresponsible parent when the school nurse rings and says there has been an accident at school, your child is distressed, and you cannot go to collect him because you are in the middle of presenting a full-day workshop, and you send your housekeeper instead.

The sensitive person will consistently have more difficulty with a fluctuating self esteem because of the greater number or adrenalin arousals that the person experiences and the larger amount of stress chemical adrenalin produced each time. Sensitive people do not "just get over" things. It is common for a sensitive person to not be over one arousing incident when the next one occurs. This results in an accumulation of adrenalin in the body, which necessarily impacts on the levels of serotonin.

Let's review what we have learned so far about Serotonin (See Chapter 1.7). Serotonin is a chemical produced in the brain for several important functions. It is the mood chemical, and elevated serotonin elevates a person's sense of well-being; hence the importance of laughter. Depleted serotonin results in a lowered mood state, also impaired thinking and impaired sleeping. Serotonin is one of the chemicals that prepare the body for sleep according to the person's sleep cycle. Significant fluctuations result in altered sleep patterns. Any stressed person knows this!

Serotonin is one of the brain's neuro-transmitters, needed to enable electrical impulses to jump across neurons in the brain, which is thought. When you are feeling down, the lowered serotonin in your brain results in the jumping coming to a halt, resulting in the brain feeling blocked or stuck or foggy. Explained simply, the electrical impulses then simply cycle in the area of the brain where they have just been, resulting in recurring thought, or dwelling. The ruminations are always about something negative, which results in the further production of adrenalin, and so the cycle of anxiety or obsessive thinking is set up, with debilitating consequences. Self-esteem and stress (negative emotion) operate as counterweights. As stress rises self-esteem decreases, and vice versa.

This is the biological cause of lowered self esteem—as serotonin lowers, thinking becomes even more inaccurate and irrational and you are unable to inject positiveness about yourself or your situation into your brain. From inside the brain, your perspective has become your reality. Without proper intervention you may ultimately become depressed. It is very difficult to "cheer up" a person who is feeling depressed, as his reality literally is an altered view of the world. Your 'inner voice' has gained control over your appraisal.

3.7 Recognize Your Inner Voice

Everyone has an inner voice. It is the conversation you have with yourself, in order to make decisions (for example, which ice-cream shall I buy?) or to discern between pain and pleasure. Sometimes it appears to be thoughts in your head, at other times a feeling without any real thought attached to it, but a feeling that you believe to be true because it is so apparent to you (for example, my partner doesn't appreciate me, he or she just takes me for granted).

It is in your consciousness, your "mind", that the identity you create for yourself—your inner view of self—is formed. Your identity consists of the events, appraisals and responses that keep you alive. The psychological structures that support and drive your identity can cause you emotional distress and/or psychological problems or they can offer you a life of EASE— You choose! The choices you have made so far have led you to where you are today. Are you a victim or victor? Are you ready to affirm an identity for yourself without judgment, without rejecting self, without an inner voice?

The inner voice is always negative and destructive, and appears louder and more vocal when a person is vulnerable and feeling stressed. People who are sensitive (those who feel their feelings with intensity) will usually have a louder inner voice than a person who "lets go" of things more quickly. The inner voice accompanies you wherever you go, and makes its presence felt in your thoughts even when uninvited. It's the voice in your head that attacks, judges, or minimizes. It can change a feeling of sheer delight or pride to one of dismay in an instant, with the result that you never feel the same strong positive feeling again, even when you do try to recapture it.

- **Case Study—Your Inner Voice Beats You Down**
  Situation: Louise, an Australian woman in her 30's, had come to Singapore with her husband six months earlier but had not found work since arriving. She decided to fulfill a long time dream of furthering her study, now that she had time, and before they had children. She enrolled in and commenced a post-graduate degree through Monash University in Victoria, Australia.

  Susan's Assessment: Louise had experienced boredom, loneliness, homesickness and a loss of self-esteem since being in Singapore. She had tried to get involved in a few activities, but felt the climate too hot (for outdoor sports) or that she was too different (no children or car) from some of the other expatriate women who lived there. She found that study was a fulfilling decision.

  Work Done In Counseling: In counseling, Louise was introduced to the concept of the inner voice as a means of helping her combat her diminished feelings of self-esteem and feelings of being different.

  Outcome: The week after being introduced to her inner voice (otherwise known as the inner critic) she was eager to tell me her story. In recent weeks, she had worked hard on her first paper for her course of study, had researched well and been pleased with her efforts. During the past week, she had obtained the results of this paper in the post. She ripped open the envelope and excitedly read that she had done very well— 87%—a distinction! She was thrilled and proud and cried "Yes" as she fisted the air with pleasure. But, she said, this great feeling lasted for only about 8 seconds. Then the voice in her head said to her, "He must have been an easy marker. Everyone else probably got a distinction as well."

- **Case Study—The Inner Voice Leaves You Indecisive Susan describes how the inner voice does its work:** Susan remembered looking patiently for a pair of sandals over a period of three to four months that suited her requirements. She wanted black strappy sandals, with a strap also at the back, in her size and within her budget. Every time Susan was at her shopping center, she looked, but there was never anything there even remotely like what she was after. That was OK. She was in no rush.

Then one day, there they were, on the shelf in the window of one of the many shoe shops at the shopping center! Just what she had been after! New stock had arrived, and she went in, tried on, and purchased a pair, all in the space of about 4 minutes. Susan was delighted, and bounced lightly out of the store with her new sandals in the box under her arm, feeling very proud about the achievement of her purchase after showing such patience. She even remembered the smile on her face and the warm feeling of pleasure. But only for about 30 seconds!

No sooner was Susan out of the store, and faced with many other stores nearby, then her inner voice was back. "You were too hasty," it said. "New stock has arrived everywhere. If you had only looked around a little bit more, you might have found these sandals for a lower price, somewhere else." Her pleasure was gone—wrecked by the critic. Even when Susan justified her rapid purchase to herself (actually to her critic) immediately afterwards,

57

and protested that her time was valuable and that she was indeed happy with what she had paid for the sandals, the critic had left her feeling dissatisfied. The pleasure was gone. The negative feelings had returned. The inner voice has done its work.

Susan's Advice For Moving Forward: Your inner voice (critic) has the ability to leave you feeling dissatisfied with any decision you make, even after you have anguished over the pros and cons for a long time. The critic takes away your ability to trust your own judgment, and the day when you had a "gut level feeling" about what to do or what to buy, seems only a distant memory. The voice is so loud in your head that that is all you hear. It becomes your only thoughts. And so you believe those thoughts to be true. They become your reality.

In counseling, you can learn to recognize your inner voice, the voice of low self-esteem, which is the first step of learning how to deal with it.

- **Case Study—Banish Low Self Esteem**

    Situation: Barry, a 37 year-old in senior management, came to counseling to explore his mood swings. He had been married for nearly six years to a "warm and wonderful person" who worked for the same company. They had arrived in Singapore only six months earlier.

    They were yet to have children, and Barry described himself as fairly conservative—certainly not a risk taker. Sometimes he couldn't believe he'd accepted a job in Singapore, as he'd never lived abroad before or visited Asia. Barry's good feelings often gave way to incredible depression and feelings of hopelessness and despair. He often felt "not good enough", "not worthy", and "not the person I thought I would turn out to be."

    Susan's Assessment: Barry's critical view of himself had escalated since arriving in Singapore. He was in a senior position and on a good salary—which he felt was too high for the work he was actually doing. He admitted that he occasionally felt suicidal. Susan identifies that Barry was suffering from lowered self-esteem. Identifying the problem was an important first step in dealing with his destructive negative emotions.

Work Done In Counseling: Barry recognised that his negative feelings were not constant. They seemed to present themselves at unpredictable times—during both work and social situations. Susan helped Barry to identify the disturbing judgmental and critical thoughts he had about himself, which were giving rise to his negative feelings. By teaching Barry strategies to cope with these negative thoughts as they arose, he was soon able to identify them and control their devastating impact.

Outcome: Barry became confident of his own abilities and recognised that he was indeed the most competent and suitable person for his job. He resumed his post-graduate studies completing a master's degree successfully within the first year of his appointment. He continued to use the self-esteem resource book suggested by Susan, *Self-Esteem*, by McKay and Fanning, as a reference tool whenever his critical inner voice arose. Most of all he felt in control of himself, his thoughts and his well being.

Susan's Advice For Moving Forward: Negative emotion can have a debilitating effect on an individual. A person will present physical, cognitive and emotional symptoms of a stress or trauma reaction. When negative emotions that arise from our critical inner voice are held within and not experienced, we can suffer lowered self-esteem and ultimately, depression. The inner voice is always negative and destructive and appears louder and more vocal when a person is vulnerable and feeling stressed. Reversing the mission of negative emotions is assisted through counseling. Precipitating thoughts are identified and reframed to create feelings of well-being that lead to raised self- esteem and self-confidence.

Physical and cognitive strategies for conquering your inner voice and elevating self-esteem are many and varied, but all are about increasing a positive or at least a realistic perspective on the situation, and preventing the cycle of anxiety or anger. Physiologically, this will prevent the production of further adrenalin, and allow time for what is already in the body to be released. No bad feeling lasts forever, if not dwelt on. This is why distraction can be very useful in the time of a stressful event.

3.8 The Breathing Square

If you happen to have a moment to spare in your trauma or in your life drama and you can think a little bit more clearly, you might like to imagine a square. Let us label this the 'breathing square'. Imagine that you are walking around this square—four steps on each side. As you are walking around the breathing square, breathe in for the count of four, hold your breath for the count of four, breathe out for four and hold your breath for four.

If you do that just three or four times, you will start to calm down as your body releases adrenalin. This technique can be done many times in any place—lying in bed trying to sleep, driving, sitting at traffic lights, sitting in an exam. Wherever you want, you can walk around the breathing square. As you are walking around the square, you are thinking present tense. When you are thinking something in the present tense and it is not threatening—and there is nothing threatening about walking around an imaginary square—you are not adding adrenalin. You will only produce adrenalin when your brain is interpreting that there is some sort of threat; when you perceive there to be some danger.

So, walking around the imaginary square is again, mimicking the way we breathe when we feel relief. As you mimic relief, the message goes straight back from your body to your brain that everything is all right. NO DANGER! The parasympathetic nervous system stops the flow of adrenalin and breath by breath you restore to calm. This is a simple, easy technique to lower your level of adrenalin—not necessarily to get back to normal, but certainly enough for you to be able to manage your thinking and be able to remain steady.

3.9 Unpack Your Negative Jigsaw

A jigsaw is a puzzle—a picture pasted on a board and cut into irregular shapes. The objective of the puzzle is to reassemble the pieces to view the picture. Generating positive emotion is being motivated to **unpack** the negative jigsaw you have assembled in your black brain through your life.

Imagine you are about to start a 1,000-piece jigsaw puzzle of your brain, but it's your black brain—the one with all the negative thoughts. When you start out in life—before you start your jigsaw—there is not much negativity. And the picture of the black brain is not even recognizable. But with every negative thought and feeling you experience you put in a few pieces. And gradually, your jigsaw starts to take shape.

When your jigsaw is half-done, there are still lots of gaps. Lots of places for positive thought and clear thinking to come through. Even when the jigsaw is three-quarters complete, there is room for rational thought—a few gaps here and there.

However, one day you wake up after a period of negative experiences, and the picture of the black brain is complete. That is your new reality—the negative brain. There is no room for anything else. From that moment on, everything that happens outside of yourself seems to reinforce your negative jigsaw—the picture of your black brain that you have pieced together. External events confirm the negative picture—the self-fulfilling prophecy.

Many of us with stressful lives start out each day with a near-completed jigsaw, a negative picture of ourselves full of negative emotion from an active and loud inner voice. To create transition, if you live life with a negative jigsaw you must learn how to unpack it—piece by piece—so that some rational thinking then has a chance to shine through.

Unpacking your negative jigsaw is another form of the 4-step cognitive framework (3.10). Each time you have a positive thought or revise a weakness (negative thought) you are removing one piece of the jigsaw. Continue to do this, one piece at a time, step-by-step, until your jigsaw is completely unpacked. As you unpack the negative thoughts in memory and fully experience the emotion associated with each thought, you are recreating your identity—your positive view of yourself. There are three ways to unpack your negative jigsaw: (1) The waterslide; (2) Repeating affirmations, and (3) The compassionate response.

It is important to note that in some people, a neuro-biological problem may exist in the brain, giving rise to negative thinking and/order precision that is not effectively managed with cognitive strategies. Instead, damage or mal-function to a particular area of the brain, may be the very cause of negative thinking, which then is dwelt on, causing a great deal of suffering to the person. In these cases, medication can be very useful to reduce inflammation/wrong activity in the brain, or to provide the "grease" for an easier shift to different thought pathways. A psychiatrist is the appropriate medical practitioner to see if the problem is neuro-biological. We discuss how to survive your depression in Chapter 4.6.

Let us now turn to the 4-step cognitive framework—a strategy to raise your emotional health.

3.10 4-Step Cognitive Framework

The 4-Step cognitive framework is a process for helping you manage your response after an emotional event by enabling you to reframe your appraisal of that event so that you achieve a better response or behavior. It will help you turn behavior you want to stop into new successful strategies to build relationships—finding just one of your annoying habits, just one small flaw, that's keeping you from being the person you want to be.

The four steps are;

1. Notice my feelings (Refer to the "feelings" word list above).
   - Close my eyes and take in some deep breaths.
   - Relax my body.
   - Notice where I feel (anger, anxiety, depressed) in my body.
2. Notice the situation – What is the upsetting (precipitating) internal or external event?
   - Ask yourself;
   - Where am I?
   - Who am I with?
   - What's happening to me?
   - What is being said or done to me?
   - What is my memory, thought, value, belief, expectation?
3. Appraisal - Automatic negative thoughts - What am I thinking?
   - Listen to the thoughts that go with the feeling in that part of my body.
   - Notice everything that I'm saying of myself.
   - Try to remember how the feeling began.
     - Distortions in thinking—Record the facts (evidence)
     - **supporting** (for) the negative thoughts?
     - Challenging the distortions—Record the facts (evidence) **negating** (against) the
     - negative thoughts?
4. Focus on thoughts more helpful (3b above) —Record your rational response.

3.11 Get Smart at Noticing Your Emotions

Emotions signal a level of need; a need for food, and water, safety, love and esteem. You don't ignore your needs—that's one reason why you've chosen to read this book. Some people do ignore their needs. They live in pain and may die from it. Others notice their need, but wait while the discomfort gets more uncomfortable, even painful, before they act. They may wait until their wants and needs are not met and endure an "Oh shit!" experience, before they decide to change their behavior.

Sometimes you find that you do not have enough energy to deal with your feelings, because your body is attempting to deal with wants and needs that lie deep inside you that are covered over while you survive life dramas. When trying to deal with these deep emotions your body becomes depleted of energy—sometimes leading to depression (See Chapter 4.6).

Don't wait for the "Oh shit!" experience. Get good at noticing emotional constipation—get good at recognizing the very first feeling of discomfort. Avoid emotional "dis-ease" by taking care of your needs at the first sign of emotional distress by creating an EAR—Identity centered in reality, not perceived reality (fantasy). Live in present moment awareness, where you experience your emotion in the present from events in the present. Discover your true identity and evaluate the role it plays in creating your emotional distress.

We have learned that emotion is a state "triggered" by an event or stimulus. The stimulus may come to you through your senses. If you can see it, hear it, taste it, smell it, or feel it on your skin or in your body, then it is real.

Perceived reality is all mental or cognitive activity—including thoughts, memories, beliefs, values, dreams and ideas. Perceived reality doesn't come <u>to</u> you. It comes <u>from</u> you. You create it using your emotional brain. If you only think it, it may be true or it may be false—but it is not real.

Emotions that are triggered in your mind, rather than by your senses, are unnecessary or optional. If you generate painful emotions by thinking negative thoughts in your mind, you will need to change how you think in order to feel better. If you create pleasurable feelings, that's great—as long as you remember that you are only using your imagination.

Sometimes you create emotions by incorrect thinking that are so strong that they cover over real feelings arising from your senses. When this happens you are "out of touch" with reality—your perceptions have become your reality. You are in danger of building resentments, clinging to unresolved hurts, and blaming others, which leads to wrong behavioral choices. Managing and resolving this emotional pain is the subject of the next chapter.

4
Manage Your Emotional Pain — Emotional Awareness Means Owning And Taking Responsibility For Your Actions

4.1 Introduction

The human body gets its primary energy from burning sugar. You get your energy from taking care of your body well—not perfectly. In fact, you only need to eat, sleep, and exercise "well enough" for your body to give you all the information you will ever need through your feelings. Feelings are "energy surges" that tell you what you need or want—food, water, safety, love, esteem, respect, understanding. When you notice these feelings, you usually have enough energy to handle the need or want they are telling you about. For example, when you feel hunger you have the energy to get up and make something to eat. But sometimes the need for sleep overrides the feeling of hunger.

Your appraisal of your thoughts produces physical manifestations that you have learned to call feelings. Feeling plus thought is experienced in the body as emotion. Emotions signal a level of need. The emotional states of anger, fear, sadness, surprise, enjoyment and disgust originate in your mind. We know that emotions can create chemical imbalances and actual toxins that cause deterioration of your body or lead to illness and pain. Pain lets you know you're alive. The way to cure the illness that you have created for yourself—the way to manage emotional pain—is to develop emotional awareness.

4.2 Develop Emotional Awareness

Awareness is the degree of clarity you have at the time you perceive, and understand, the need at hand. You will always choose an action that seems most likely to meet your need at the time. The potential benefits of the action you choose might seem—at least at the time—to outweigh the foreseeable disadvantages. For example, you may choose anger as a payback for a hurt you feel. This may meet your need, but is possibly an inappropriate response because of the impact of your anger on the other person.

As you recognise and understand your needs and wants—and despair that they are not being met—you become open to thoughts and feelings that are mostly painful. You may have a 'light bulb' moment—when everything suddenly becomes clear to you—and begin to ask yourself, "Why is everything going wrong? Why am I feeling forsaken? Why am I feeling rejected? Why am I always angry? Why am I treated so badly? Why did he or she leave me? What's wrong with my behavior? Why am I so depressed?" Sooner or later your stored hurts and resentments will overwhelm you.

When you begin to ask yourself these questions, you are developing emotional awareness. You are recognising and examining major physiological and psychological problems in your body. People who don't ask themselves these questions simply blame others for the discomfort they feel. Their emotional constipation remains. This is because in blaming others and not owning your feelings you are giving someone else the *responsibility* for your feelings. The bad news is, *you* are responsible for *your* actions in that you will inevitably pay the price—willing or not, consciously or unconsciously—for your lack of awareness. The good news is you can choose to change how you feel!

Becoming emotionally aware means owning and taking responsibility for your actions—knowing the price you pay for your actions. It's worth the effort because low emotional awareness means that you are later surprised—even dismayed—at the cost of some of your decisions.

- **Case Study—Blaming**

    Mia and Barry were on holidays on the Gold Coast with their two small boys, and staying in a lovely hotel near the beach. It was just as Mia had wanted and she was very happy with the way their holiday was going. Barry was pleased that Mia was happy, as she tended to get irritated at the smallest thing, and he usually got the blame for things that went wrong.

    Mia got things ready for the full day's outing at Dreamworld, an amusement park, the next day. She checked the camera and remarked to Barry that the battery was low and that she must charge it before going to bed. Mia was the photographer in the family and took pride in her photos and her equipment.

    The next day, at the entrance of Dreamworld, just after they had bought the tickets, Mia remembered the camera. She realized the battery had not been put on the charger and immediately got upset, as this of course would limit the number of photos she could take that day. She was mad at Barry for not doing it when she mentioned it the night before. When Barry mentioned that he never did it and that she always did it "so that it was done right", Mia was still mad at Barry for not reminding her about it before she went to bed. Mia yelled that she had told Barry about the battery being low so that he could remind her to do it. And when Barry did not say he was sorry, Mia got even madder, screaming at Barry that he didn't love her, and if he did he would have recharged the battery himself or at least reminded her to do it. Surely he could have seen that she had so many things on her mind, preparing for their big day!

    The situation got so out of hand and Mia was so distressed

about the camera that she refused to go into Dreamworld, yelling at Barry that they would have to return to the hotel and make plans to come back to Dreamworld on another occasion. Barry tried to console Mia and reminded her that their family ticket was for use on that day only. Their experience at the theme park, he told Mia, was more valuable than the photos. This did not console Mia at all and she remained upset that Barry didn't understand her and "you have no idea what's important to me". Meanwhile the boys were becoming upset at their mother's outburst and restless and whining because they wanted to get going in Dreamworld.

The outcome was not good. Barry took the boys into the park by himself, and Mia returned to the hotel by taxi (more expense, but that too was described as Barry's "own fault") to recharge the battery. The fact that a family's day outing had been destroyed was viewed by Mia as entirely Barry's fault. At no time could she accept the responsibility for not having recharged the battery or regulate her mood sufficiently to recover from her disappointment about the photos, in order to not create disappointment for the others over aborted plans.

When Barry tried to point this out to Mia, he was told that if he, Barry, had gone along with her plans to return to the hotel, then everything would have been alright. Again, Barry was blamed for the situation having not worked out according to Mia's plans.

Whilst Mia chose actions that seemed to meet your need at the time, which was to release the increased adrenalin in her body due to her irritation and frustration that the camera had not been charged, her blaming behavior in turn impacted adversely on Barry and the children, ruining what should have been a wonderful family day out.

4.3 Pain Perception and Arousal

In Chapter 1 we described how pain perception is about how appraisal triggers arousal (emotional response) in your body. Deepak Chopra explains that cognitive appraisal in the brain arouses only two impulses—pain or pleasure.

> We all want to avoid pain and experience pleasure. Therefore, all the complicated emotional states we find ourselves in are because we are unable to obey these basic drives. [5]

Pleasure seems to be managed well by most people and is a non-problem status. Pain though is any unpleasant sensory and emotional experience. Acute pain is a normal sensation triggered in the autonomic nervous system to alert you to a possible injury. Chronic pain refers to discomfort relating to injury, disease or emotional distress. Chronic pain persists and may exist in the absence of any past physical injury or body damage. Examples of chronic pain include; arthritis pain, cancer pain, headache, lower back (coccyx) pain, and pain from damage to the central nervous system itself.

Although pain affects your body's responsiveness, its overall impact on you lies within you. Your perceptions therefore, are crucial in pain management.

All pain is felt in the body in the present—today. You cannot physically feel something yesterday or tomorrow. You can remember the pain of the past or anticipate a pain in the future, but you can only feel pain in the present.

- **For example;**

    Where were you, what did you feel, and what you do when you first heard the news of the September 11, 2001 disaster in New York, USA—the October 12, 2002 bombing in Bali, Indonesia—the train bombing in Madrid, Spain on March 11, 2004? What did you feel over the next two to three days after each event? Did your body feel normal? What do you feel today when you recall those events?

All emotion is felt in the present at various levels of intensity; low, medium and high. Each time you experience a negative emotion—such as a hurt in the present, anger or resentment from a memory of the past, or fear and anxiety from perceived pain in the future—you are adding to your store of stress. The stronger (higher the intensity) you feel an emotion in your body, the greater the amount of stress and adrenalin that accumulates in your body.

Pain felt in the body can be depicted on a **pain time-line**.

Chopra explains the cycle of emotions that begins in the present (reality)—where only pain and pleasure are felt—and ends in complex emotions centered exclusively in the past, such as, guilt and depression (our perceived reality).

71

The cycle that gets repeated countless times in everyone's life is as follows:

- Pain in the present is experienced as hurt.

- Pain in the past is remembered as anger. Anger starts with an internal or external event and is the subjective experience of physiological arousal (stress response) to negative appraisal of the event.

- Pain in the future is perceived as anxiety—a lessening of mental relaxation, associated to the alert reaction. Fear, and its manifestation, anxiety, is a painful emotion caused by impending danger or an evil event—a state of alarm, dread of something, or anxiety (extreme worry) over life changes.

- Unexpressed anger—redirected against yourself and held within—is called guilt.

- The depletion of energy that occurs when anger is redirected inward creates depression. We include a section on surviving depression later in this chapter (see Chapter 4.6).

The cycle of emotion tells us that stored hurt is something we all have experience of to some degree, and is responsible for considerable adrenalin arousal. Chopra says, "Buried hurt disguises itself as anger, anxiety, guilt, and depression." To live in the present we need to learn to avoid the easy emotion—anger, and deal with the hurt that is more difficult to confront. Unresolved anger will only grow worse, feeding on itself.

Sometimes you can cause another person pain by what you do or say. This external event may be intentional or unintentional, and may also create a pain for you; guilt, remorse, shame, and regret—that is, stress. For example, people who use ineffective communication (Chapter 5.6) often drag up "history" in arguments to hurt their partner. Their perception is that their partner has hurt them or is "blaming" them in some way. They are using a conditioned response, to ease their own pain felt in the present—not realising the physiological impact their behaviour is having on their own body.

Pain is communicated to others through language, posture, withdrawal, and abuse, including physical, emotional, and sexual abuse. In an integrated model of the cognitive, affective, and physiological aspects of emotion, pain is manifested as negative emotion (accumulated stress) and can lead to nervous illness.

The physical and psychological effects of accumulated stress (pain) felt in the body have been reported (Chapters 1.7 and 1.8). Let's review them here;

1. A breakdown in the immune system.
2. An interruption to the autonomic nervous system.
3. A decrease in the level of the hormone serotonin in the brain.
4. Lowered self-esteem – which may lead to depression.

The sole function of fear, anxiety or anger is to stop stress, to stop pain. We know that how we feel depends on how we think. Fear, anxiety and anger therefore arise from our thoughts and are felt as stress in our body. The thoughts that give rise to fear, anxiety or anger can be changed so that we no longer feel the pain. Changing the way we think and our mood (attitude) through increased awareness is the only conscious control we have—other than medication—to stop pain. Our behavior modification tool, EAR—Identity, using the 4-step cognitive framework (Chapter 3.10), will help you effectively change the way you think and ease your pain. Other treatment for pain includes; medication, acupuncture, surgery, relaxation therapy, yoga, and psychotherapy.

If you are experiencing emotional pain, and have a *reactive* emotional style, you need to move from anger to assertion. If you have an *avoidant* emotional style you need to set as your goal to move from fear to appreciation.

4.4 From Anger to Assertion—Paul Robbins

Early in 1993, after successfully graduating with a Bachelor of Theology degree the previous year, and in anticipation of continuing to complete two fi years of post-graduate study in pastoral ministry, I received a letter from the principal of the seminary I had attended. He wrote to advise me that a decision had been made some two years earlier by the seminary faculty, that I be excluded from public ministry. This decision, up until then, had never been communicated to me. It was revealed only after I had applied for readmission to the post-graduate course.

The deceit and betrayal I felt was bewildering and heart-wrenching. After four years of study I felt deceived, betrayed, angry and humiliated. Knowing that this decision had been withheld from me triggered an angry response within me. I wrote a letter of protest to the president of the church, complaining about the way the decision had been made without consultation. After a three-month delay, the president issued me with a one-line reply, "We are sorry you see things the way you do." Susan and I felt totally dismissed, disrespected, abandoned, and helpless.

I felt my rejection by the church very keenly. It was a source of enormous pain. What hurt the most was their challenge to my integrity. I had committed me and my family to the vocation of pastoral ministry. I became consumed by the psychological trauma of trust that had been betrayed. What followed was four years of unemployment, a substantial loss of income, severe stress headaches, and a general deterioration in health, as I began the long road back to normalcy. During most of this period I grieved over my loss of opportunity for public ministry—something that at the time, I felt called upon by God to do. Instead, I had to deal with my anger, rejection, loss of face, and severe lowered self-esteem.

My inner voice took over from the 'men of the church' and became my critic;

- "How could they do this to Susan and me?"
- "Why won't they talk to us about it? You are too set in your ways – they are threatened by you."
- "You wouldn't have made a good pastor anyway."
- "They didn't really want you anyway Paul. You're not one of them!"

After four years of trying to deal with the pain, my doctor—who well knew my emotional pain and psychological state—said to me, "Paul, you are the one displaying the symptoms. Everyone else has moved on." He was referring to the symptoms of stress and negativity I felt in my body. He referred me to a psychologist who taught me to slow down, get to know my inner voice, and start working on the four-step process to reframe the negative messages in my head, pounding away day and night. My psychologist helped me to accept that the men who ran the church—and who had failed to counsel me about their decision to exclude me from the ministry, nor had they subsequently acknowledged my pain of rejection—were doing the best they could, given their level of awareness at the time. My doctor told me, "You are talking to the wrong kind of people!" At last here was a path forward.

After four years I finally realized that what I had seen in the 'men of the church', who had disenfranchised me from the public ministry, I had failed to see in myself. My perception (appraisal) of the 'men of the church' was a mirror of what was going on inside of me. I alone was responsible for my emotional distress, not the men of the church. I blamed them for excluding me from public ministry. And I had projected my angry feelings onto them. They had the problem, not me, I believed! And I was going to let them know. Who did they think they were? They couldn't treat me like this—without respect and without affirming my right of consultation. But this attitude only fuelled my anger. I saw in the pastors and presidents of the church what I failed to see in myself. I had determined that the men of the church were 'the enemy'. But the real enemy was within me. My perception justified my need for vindication. And my response was anger. Finally I realized the lesson in this terrible experience—I was the one who made me angry, no one else!

In turning my loss of ministry in on myself I chose to deal with my pain as I had been conditioned to act. My response to a perceived attack on my integrity was anger. The chain of emotions I experienced—anger, disrespect, abandonment and guilt—led to lowered self esteem and depression. My automatic response had been the conditioned response of a reactive person dealing with pain. My anger was a reflection of my own appraisal of events. In seeking to ease my pain, I had chosen anger over assertion. I had given away my power and opted for victim- hood over a life of ease. My need for vindication (an at triggered an appraisal that set off a reactive response (anger) in me. This is how a reactive person deals inappropriately with pain, until they let go of past conditioning.

I used the cognitive-behavioral strategies, now encapsulated in this book and our earlier book, *Emotional Leadership. Using emotionally intelligent behaviour to enjoy a life of ease,* to deal with my cognitive appraisals and emotional constipation. Slowly, I put the pieces together unpacking my black brain and began the long road back. My self-esteem returned after focusing on my considerable achievements. I completed an MBA degree, a PhD in emotional intelligence, and became a visiting lecturer in a Polytechnic in Singapore. I operated my own very successful human support organization with Susan in Singapore for 12 years, now based on the Gold Coast, Australia.

I do not condone what was done to Susan and me by the 'men of the church'. It forever changed my trust in organized religion—but not in my spirituality. However, had I been able to manage my emotion better at the time, and used the 4-step cognitive framework, I would have seen immediately that I was the one displaying the symptoms. I was the one talking to the wrong kind of people. It would have saved me a lot of pain and time. It took four years for me to learn that there is another, easier, way to deal with deep-rooted anger—simply change your attitude, belief, value, or expectation. A change of perception would have generated a different response to my experience, namely, assertion.

In experiencing deep anger about my dismissal for ministry, I learned the truth of Aldous Huxley's words, "Experience is not what happens to you; it is what you do with what happens to you." I challenged my EAR—Identity and thereby aspects of my personality. I moderated my need for vindication (for truth) by rising from my point of view to my viewing point. I became more tolerant of ambiguity.

As events happen to me today, at the age of 62, I am still a person with a reactive emotional style, but one who uses the 'gap' between event and response to moderate my behavior. I choose to sit on my hands, take time-out, draw on my emotional intelligence, the 4-square breathing technique, and the 4-step cognitive framework to generate positive emotion to balance the stress felt in my body. I process events into action in present moment awareness to increase my joy of living.

The benefit of the professional and medical assistance I received was that it helped me to understand how I could deal with my emotional pain and find healing in my life. This help gave me hope. The advice helped trigger a compassionate response in me. Transformation fi began by forgiving the men who had been—or so it had seemed—dismissive of me.

Relax Release Let go reminds me of my essential purpose—to love and be loved. Life is for making memories. The events that cause me pain—those that I experience in unawareness—are the events I learn the most from. Make the choice, as I did, to be free from past conditioning, free to heal your life.

Many of you will be motivated to change by your experience of pain. Others will hold onto the agitation and irritation in your lives driven by the fear of not surviving. Life has a habit of holding us hostage to our lack of awareness. Only a fool is totally secure about himself. At the right moment the teacher will appear to help you release your pain.

As you begin your journey of emotional awareness you may find your path blocked. You will find that the central impediment to change has been *you*. You will be overwhelmed by your character defects and low level of emotional ability. Take heart—this is the beginning of meaningful change.

I chose assertion over anger. Using the strategies in this book, I learned to manage my response after an emotional event. This required an inner change of attitude; from anger and a need for vindication to a life fully lived as an emotionally intelligent person.

Expert on Asian wisdom, Chin-Ning Chu (1992), wrote;

> 'Transformation' has no fixed formula. It results from your willingness to do battle within, and your unceasing courage to cultivate inner strength to overcome your liabilities. Through this self-cultivation, you will eventually produce the magical fruit that will transform your attitudes in every aspect of your life.[6]

My advice for moving forward:

> Life is for making memories. What you do should come from your desire to live fully—rather than from reasoning (explaining) and arguing (complaining) to justify yourself. Self-acceptance is releasing other people's opinions about you. Never let others' opinions affect your view of yourself. Always act with compassion toward others—be understanding, accepting and forgiving. Surround yourself with people who make you feel good—and leave the rest in the dust of your victories!"

4.5 From Fear to Appreciation Susan Robbins

I have always understood my feelings and articulated them well. As young as 14-years of age, I remember my mother telling me to "stop analysing everything". I was constantly thinking, interpreting, discussing or journaling the things that I felt.

I am a sensitive person with an avoidant emotional style. My parents never displayed conflict. And the message my siblings and I consistently heard was, "If you haven't got anything nice to say, then don't say anything at all." My nature and conditioning resulted in an innate and learned disability of not knowing how to behave in a conflict situation. The first person in my life to yell at me was my husband, Paul!

Early in our communication, if the tone of Paul's voice indicated that he was irritated or frustrated, I would interpret that as him being mad or angry with me. Feeling wounded and misunderstood, my response was to simply withdraw. I thought that withdrawing was the 'correct' thing to do. And I'd wait for an apology from Paul, who had 'lost his cool' and hurt my feelings. I had done nothing wrong after all! I had certainly not said anything that was not nice.

I believed that Paul would know that I was a caring, calm and loving person, and that I would not deliberately irritate or frustrate him. If only he would simply tell me what the problem was—in a quiet and respectful tone—I would not only listen gladly, but I would also be very willing to change my behavior so he was not so upset.

I experience conflict as extreme anxiety in my body. Without any doubt, conflict, raised voices, and sarcastic tones cause my body to become extremely aroused—in a negative way. Initially I thought that all people experienced this physical response. Even hearing people using raised or angry voices in another room can set off this physical response in me. Understanding this now, I realize that this is the reason I seek harmony in my environment wherever possible—at home, or work, or in my personal relationships. "Be pleasant, talk in a normal voice", I can hear myself requesting of others. I will usually avoid conflict—rather than deal with it—in an attempt to minimize the arousal I experience in a situation of conflict.

After the events of September 11, 2001 in the USA, my body manifestations escalated. On that day, I felt terror like I had not known it before. In the days that followed September 11—especially as I counseled those affected personally by the tragedy—I became flooded with negative feelings. They were most irrational—but they were there nonetheless. During that time I felt; fearful, alarmed, trapped, unsafe, restricted, constrained, lost, inadequate, helpless, powerless, controlled, and anxious.

From that time on I became more irritable and short-tempered, frazzled and sometimes withdrawn. The smallest stress would set me off. My heart always seemed to be pounding and my chest racing. Any irritability displayed by Paul or the children would set a reaction off in me. I felt as though Paul should know what I was going through and try to be considerate of my feelings. I was often grumpy and would snap back at others.

My adrenalin was near saturation level. I recognized the feelings as anxiety, but I couldn't determine what I was so anxious about. Were terrorists coming to Singapore, where I was living at the time? Not likely. Yet I would wake in the morning with my heart pounding. It was just getting ridiculous!

I decided to try herbal medication to alleviate the physical symptoms. I found that calming tablets from the pharmacy helped to take the edge off the distressing sensations in my body. This not only helped me to remain focused during the day, but it also assisted me in getting a much better sleep at night. What I learned by this experiment with such calming medications was that my over-active mind was my own worst enemy. It kept me awake many nights with swirling thoughts.

Then in quick succession I read two amazing books; *The Highly Sensitive Person* by Elaine Aron (1997)[7] and *Peace From Nervous Suffering* by Dr Claire Weekes (1972)[8]. In both books I experienced astonishment, the "Oh my God, this is me" reaction, as I read about the physical manifestations associated with arousal as experienced by the sensitised person.

An explanation at last! This was real—it wasn't "just in my head". I truly felt the stress chemical adrenalin in my body. This now explained my tendency to withdraw, to become speechless, to instinctively want distance during times of emotional pain in a relationship. And it also explained why I needed time to "warm up" following an argument. As a reactive person, Paul always recovered much faster than me and often believed I was 'punishing' him by responding slowly with warmth and affection. Weekes (1972, p. 7) writes;

> Our feelings become calm because we change our mood. Changing mood (attitude) is the only conscious control— other than medication—we have over our involuntary nerves, and so over our symptoms of stress.

Since exploring the explanation of adrenalin and nervous suffering—and the techniques to manage first and second stages of fear once I recognize the state of arousal—I have understood even more about myself. The adage, "You are responsible for your own feelings" now registers as true. It is *my* body that feels these sensations, these pains. The thoughts that are associated with the pain are mine too—the irrational, anxious and blaming thoughts. Often these thoughts interpret the intentions or actions of others inaccurately. For example, when Paul would raise his voice to staff in a shop I would feel, "Paul is embarrassing me". In reality, I realize that he would not deliberately embarrass me, nor hurt me in any way. He loves me. I have mountains of evidence of that.

Yes, I may *feel* embarrassed—but Paul is not embarrassing me. Through blaming or "projecting out" my feelings it seems that Paul is embarrassing me. In fact, I am seeing in Paul what I have failed to see in myself—I am having thoughts of "I feel embarrassed", and the arousal I feel in my body comes from my own thoughts.

I can now separate the feelings and judgmental, blaming thoughts, and work solely on reducing my arousal state by maintaining a positive mental attitude. In August 2002 I went to have some energy rebalancing done in order to clear the negative energies surrounding me. I felt validated to learn that the vast number of electro-magnetic devices we use today bombard our personal energy fields—causing feelings of stress and negativity. I also learned ways to strengthen and retain the positive experiences that I have.

Now, everyone is benefiting—the children, Paul, friends, our clients, and most of all me! I feel much more "in control". Through experiencing my pain I know that I have finely tuned my body even better than before, and I am not beholden to it. I may still experience the arousal state, but I am able to manage it—I am in charge! And for that I feel settled, which is the state in which I function best. So now I can create that settled state whenever the need arises.

I chose appreciation over fear. Using the strategies in this book, I learned to manage my response after an emotional event and now enjoy family, friends, clients, and a life of ease over fear, anxiety, and nervous illness.

One of the inevitable consequences of someone allowing a debilitating inner voice beat you up or choosing not to move from anger to assertion or from fear to appreciation is that you will have significantly altered the chemical balance in your brain. This may lead to adrenalin levels in your body rising beyond your optimal level, resulting in depression. It is the mission of your inner voice to bring you down, to lead you into depression. How then, do you survive this pain?

4.6 Stress + Stress + Stress = Depression

Relentless stress—negative emotion—can lead to depression, but not always. The accumulation of stress chemicals (adrenalin) in your system results in a reduction in your level of serotonin. We said earlier that serotonin is a chemical required by your brain to maintain your sense of well-being and to assist your thinking. Depression is now known to be an imbalance of these chemicals.

Yet not everyone experiencing relentless stress will become depressed. Depression is not an automatic consequence if life is tough for a while. It is often a sense of disconnection with others that can be the determining factor. This is why loneliness can be a trigger for depression, especially in the elderly. The quality of our community and relationships can determine whether a person in a stressful environment has the capacity to cope with major life challenges, or will eventually become depressed.

The genocide in Cambodia during the late 1970's resulted in many people suffering depression to this day, thirty years on. Why? Because the regime destroyed family groups and forced a loss of community. The Khmer Rouge separated children from parents and dragged children apart. People were not allowed to talk to members of their family and family members were set against one another so that no one could trust anyone else. The very fabric of what makes a community and what helps people to maintain hope and will was calculatedly destroyed, and with it, a population descended into depression. Only now, two generations on, with the growth of new families and the development of new relationships, are people regaining hope and strength.

It is very important to recognize that with the chemical imbalance of depression comes the alteration of thinking. Serotonin is not just our mood chemical but also our thinking chemical, so when you are depressed your thinking becomes inaccurate and irrational. Your reality changes. Again, this can be explained biologically.

Serotonin is a neurotransmitter in your brain and aids the jumping of electrical impulses across the neurons. This is the basic mechanism of thought. So with the depletion of serotonin, less jumping occurs and thought is impaired. The electrical impulses halt, and do not jump any further, reducing your ability for idea association and creative thinking. Instead, the impulses simply go around in the area of the brain where they have just been—resulting in dwelling or rumination.

We only dwell when we feel bad, so the thought we have over and over and over is always a bad thought. In response, the body produces more adrenalin and we become more anxious, more stressed, and our serotonin is further depleted. It literally becomes a vicious cycle. This is why you can get to the point where you may be unable to recover by yourself and may benefit from taking some medication, to help the elevation of serotonin.

4.7 Surviving Your Depression

Depression is an illness, and often a serious one. Being depressed feels like living under a black cloud that never lifts, where all hope and joy is gone. Nothing is fun and nothing is meaningful. Your emotions are dulled and you can't respond normally to the people who love and care about you. Your relationships and your job fall apart—and it doesn't matter much to you. It's all you can do to drag yourself out of bed each day, and sometimes you can't even do that. You couldn't care less if you live or die. In its extreme form, clinical depression requires medical intervention.

Depression is not the same thing as sadness. There's much more to it. Any of the following can be part of a depressive illness:

- Feeling sad, crying easily
- Sleep disturbance
- Changes in appetite and weight
- Loss of interest and motivation

- Loss of energy, fatiguing quickly
- Physical aches and pains, especially headache and abdominal pain
- Loss of sexual interest, impotence
- Feelings of helplessness
- Guilt, self-reproach
- Pessimism regarding the future
- Irritability
- Anxiety and panic attacks
- Confusion, poor memory
- Attempts to treat the symptoms with alcohol or drug abuse

Signs of a depressed mood include[9]:

- Lowered self-esteem (or self-worth)
- Change in sleep patterns, that is, insomnia or broken sleep
- Changes in appetite or weight
- Less ability to control emotions such as pessimism, anger, guilt, irritability and anxiety
- Varying emotions throughout the day, for example, feeling worse in the morning and better as the day progresses
- Reduced capacity to experience pleasure: you can't enjoy what's happening now, nor look forward to anything with pleasure. Hobbies and interests drop off.
- Reduced pain tolerance: you are less able to tolerate aches and pains and may have a host of new ailments
- Changed sex drive: absent or reduced
- Poor concentration and memory: some people are so impaired that they think that they are going demented
- Reduced motivation: it doesn't seem worth the effort to do anything, things seem meaningless
- Lowered energy levels.

If you have such feelings and they persist for most of every day for two weeks or longer, and interfere with your ability to manage at home and at work, then you might benefit from getting an assessment by a skilled professional.

Having one or other of these features, by themselves, is unlikely to indicate depression; however there could be other causes which may warrant medical assessment. If you are feeling suicidal it is very important to seek immediate help, preferably by a mental health practitioner.

The expression "I'm so depressed" is overused and misused, and tends to undermine just how debilitating a condition real depression can be. It is important to make the distinction between sadness and depression, and to acknowledge that it is rare for normal sadness to lead to depression. Normal sadness occurs when you experience great loss, for example. At these times, the normal response is grief, which is intense, and can last weeks or months, but eventually has a resolution. Certainly if there are other factors, such as a genetic predisposition or unhelpful personal coping skills, these events might place you at a greater risk of depression. But most people who suffer sadness do not become depressed.

In life there is also disappointment and anguish. None of us is as good as we wish to be and life doesn't consistently deliver us the things we hope for. We struggle with relationships and with our work, and can become very unhappy about things not achieved. We can agonize about the difficulties we face and have regrets about decisions we have made. But none of this is depression either.

It is very hard for someone to admit, "I don't actually know why I am depressed." It is human nature to want the events we experience to explain our emotional state, and so we often say that our depression was caused by, say, our marriage breakup or loss of job. But very often we find that the depression was there long before the event took place. It may in fact have been the cause of the marriage breakup or job loss.

It is entirely possible that you can experience depression, or a lowered mood state, and not even recognize that you are depressed. There may or may not be events that cause you to feel down, but you say to yourself, "Yes, I know I'm feeling a bit down and I must do something about it. It is not good to go around feeling like this." And so the days and the weeks can go by, you feel almost constantly stressed and anxious, you have no energy, you don't go out except to work and even there you keep to yourself. Your appetite drops, you don't sleep well. You find yourself waking during the night. You feel sad and cry easily, and find your eyes brimming with tears often and unpredictably. You find you cannot concentrate well, you can't make decisions, and your memory sometimes fails you. You may have headaches or muscle aches. You tell yourself you should do some exercise, but you can't be bothered. You often have a loss of energy and become easily fatigued. Everything is an effort. You are aware of your lack of interest and motivation and hope that you will soon 'snap out of it.'

You are experiencing the symptoms of depression and are unaware of it. It never even occurs to you that you may have depression because you are usually such a steady and positive person. The thought of *you* having depression does not even cross your mind! But depression is not a weakness. It is not something to be ashamed of. It is an illness that can be treated.

- **Case Study—Lowered Mood State**

    Susan accompanied Malcolm to the doctor for an assessment of alcoholism. His recent bouts of drinking had caused him to be verbally and physically abusive toward his wife, who had finally ordered him out of the house with an ultimatum: "Get help or get out of my life." He had sought counseling to help him dry out and get his life back on track.

    The first thing the doctor inquired into was his mood state.

"On a scale of zero to ten," the doctor asked, "where zero is the worst and ten is the best feeling you can have, what do you usually feel?"

"Oh, about a three," Malcolm answered. "But sometimes I can get up to a seven or an eight.'

The doctor then asked, "And how long have you felt at about a three?"

"Four months," he replied, "and I think that is why I have been drinking more, to drown my sorrows."

"Then we must treat your depression before we do anything else," the doctor said.

Malcolm was taken aback look at the situation. "But I'm not depressed. I still get up and go to work to support my family."

The doctor explained, "You have a lowered mood state. Yes, it fluctuates. It can go up and then down again, but for the most part, you exist below a fi e. You are meant to feel higher than fi e most of the time, and so if you feel lower than a fi e for more than three consecutive weeks, it is time to get some outside help. This is because the ability to 'pull yourself together' has eluded you and you can no longer do it on your own."

Malcolm had not recognized he was depressed and felt better for the explanation. He had been beating himself up for not being able to get himself out of the doldrums, and he also beat himself up for his excessive drinking. So had his wife. Now they both had a new and more hopeful and productive way to look at the situation.

4.8 Treatment for Depression

Treatment for depression depends on several factors: the severity of your illness, what types of symptoms you have, and for how long you have had them. For some, counseling and learning cognitive techniques to alter negative thinking is sufficient for them to begin to recover. Others need to engage in activities and do something, volunteer or part-time work, for example, in order to find a feeling of connection and purpose.

For others, anti-depressant medication is a good option and should be discussed with your doctor. On medication, a person will usually begin to feel better within two or three weeks after starting medication, and will find it easier to cope with his or her day-to-day routines. If the person has been low on serotonin for some time, he or she may feel the difference within just a matter of days.

A combination of medication and counseling is considered the preferred option so that once the chemicals are restored, the person can use learned cognitive techniques to maintain the balance. It is all a matt of keeping the chemicals in equilibrium.

4.9 To Medicate or Not to Medicate

Many of you may of course be concerned that anti-depressants will turn you into a zombie and that you will be 'artificially happy', and not really you. There is also a common concern expressed about becoming reliant on, or addicted to, the medication and it being addictive.

Anti-depressants are not addictive, and the purpose of starting them is so that you can eventually come off them. The aim is to have your chemicals back in balance as quickly as possible so that your mood is raised and your thinking becomes again more rational. One does not *have* to take medication, but medication fast-forwards the recovery process—it's like going to a party on the fifteenth floor, and making a choice between taking the lift or the stairs. Both will get you to the same place, but the stairs will take longer, you will suffer exhaustion along the way, and you will have missed out on most of the fun by the time you get there.

The most common anti-depressants are Selective Serotonin Re-uptake Inhibitors (SSRIs), which work by inhibiting or reducing the rate of reabsorption of your serotonin. The easiest analogy is to describe an instant water heater. The water that flows into a water heater remains in the heater long enough to heat up, then flows out as hot water is required. If it has not been in the heater long enough, the water is only lukewarm. It is ineffective. Similarly, serotonin is produced in the body and needs to remain in the brain for a sufficient time to be used effectively for mood and for thought. In the presence of adrenalin, serotonin "flows out" of the brain (is reabsorbed) too quickly to be of benefit, resulting in low mood and impaired thinking. An anti-depressant medication (SSRI) slows down the reabsorption process leaving serotonin "dammed up" in the brain, for mood and thought.

4.10 Medication Myths

Because so many people feel that taking medication is a sign of weakness, or have had negative experiences with medication other than anti-depressants, there are a lot of opinions and misconceptions in general conversations on the topic. Let's address them one by one.

Misconception: I don't need it. I can do it on my own.

Truth: You can't, you've tried. You've done your best already.
Misconception: It shows weakness of character.

Truth: Depression is an illness. The illness makes you weak.
Misconception: Medication is addictive.

Truth: Anti-depressant medication is not addictive. Here is a chart to explain the difference.

Addictive substance:

- Gives you a high when you take it, e.g. Ecstasy.
- You need more and more of it to achieve the same effect.

- Withdrawal from the substance causes problems.
- You will spend the rest of your life looking for it.

Anti-depressant:

- Does not give you a high; rather it calms you down.
- You don't need more and more of it.
- You get to your recommended dose and then stay on it for as long as you need, and then reduce.
- Withdrawal too quickly may cause problems so follow the doctor's advice. You will then come off it and say, "I hope I never need that again."
- You will not spend your life wanting to go back on it. Rather, now you know the symptoms of depression/anxiety you will avoid getting so low in the future.

Misconception: Medication will dull my brain.

Truth: Anti-depressants usually enable you to think more clearly. The ability to smell, taste, and see more clearly has also been reported.

Misconception: Once you start you cannot stop.

Truth: The idea of starting is so that you may eventually stop.
Misconception: If you stop the medication, you will relapse.

Truth: With some illnesses, yes. With depression, not often. The medication alters and corrects the imbalance of chemicals in the brain so that you no longer have the illness. Understanding your illness and its symptoms assists you to prevent the situation recurring in the future, using cognitive strategies.

- **Case Study—Not the Real Me**

    Situation: Susan was seeing a young woman Nat, who worked as a horse trainer, and who had been involved in a freak work accident. One of the horses leapt against and then on top of her after being startled, resulting in the woman suffering a broken leg. She had complications with the setting of her leg and then with infection beneath the cast. For months Nat was off work, away from her social support and her beloved horses. She replayed the accident over and over in her mind, trying to think of how it happened and what she should have done differently. She was normally so "in tune" with the horses that she felt she should have intuited the danger. She started to doubt herself and her ability to work with horses again. Her sleep became disturbed as she often had nightmares of being crushed by the horse, and she completely lost her appetite, her weight dropping dramatically. As she was unable to work, she spent most of her time at home alone with her dogs, and became more and more resistant to going out with friends even when they did ask, citing her immobility as the reason. In the end they stopped asking, and whilst relieved, she started to feel isolated and abandoned.

    Work Done In Counseling: When Nat started counseling, she could not tell her story without crying. She cried at every sentence, and started to shake and sweat as she was forced to relive the trauma. Then she would apologize for crying, stating this was "not the real me". Nat explained that she was usually a busy and active outdoors person, and this accident has changed her from an outgoing a positive person to someone who was "pathetic", "skinny", "unsociable", "hopeless", "useless" and a "nuisance" (her husband had commented that she was not the person he had married and she interpreted this as her being a nuisance to him, now that he had to look after all the household chores as well as look after her). Nat was also fearful that she would never "get back to how I was".

Susan noted the symptoms and the fact that Nat's accident had been some months earlier. She normalised Nat's emotions but said, Enough! Susan told Nat that she had suffered a trauma and that it was evident that the ramifications of the accident were that she now suffered depression. Initially Nat was resistant to this suggestion and declined any suggestion of medication. After a few more weeks of disturbed sleep, nightmares, poor concentration, inability to get involved with life, Nat finally agreed to "give medication a go". Within a week of starting her SSRI, Nat could feel the difference. Whilst not yet feeling on top of the world, Nat said that the "edge" of her anxiety and distress had been taken away, and that her sleep was better. With better sleep came better feelings and an ability to think about things differently—and more rationally. She agreed to go out socially with her husband and started to take a bit more interest in her appearance, having her hair cut and styled, and putting on a bit of makeup for the first time in months. Whilst her misshapen leg still caused her distress, she began to wear long skirts to hide the disfigurement.

Outcome: Having forgotten to fill her scripts prior to Christmas, Nat ran out of her SSRI over the Christmas period, but as she felt so much better, believed she no longer needed them, and that it was OK to go without for the few days over Christmas. She felt the difference within two days, however, and wished she had not gone off the tablets "cold turkey". She told Susan she had felt panicky and restless and quite confused in her thinking, and could only put it down to the cessation of medication. She then feared recommencing the tablets in case she became addicted!

Susan's Advice For Moving Forward: Susan explained that Nat needed to resume the medication for a while longer yet, to assist her to think rationally and with reality. Susan also explained the importance of weaning off the drugs as directed by the doctor, not to abruptly stop. This was so the effects of coming off the drugs could be monitored and medication adjusted as the person's body made allowances to the lowered dosage. Once a person no longer needs an SSRI, because the chemicals are rebalanced, there is no benefit to staying on the SSRI and he/she can start to wean off slowly. In doing so, the person will not notice any change—their chemicals are back to normal. In Nat's case, her ceasing the SSRI medication was too premature and she needed to recommence them to combat her depression and impaired thinking.

Usually depression occurs when you turn your negative emotion in on yourself. However, there are many times when people blame others for their negative emotion. This results in a build up of resentments which cause emotional pain and need to be resolved.

5
Communicate Effectively — The Key to Any Relationship

5.1 Introduction

Good communication is the foundation stone for mutually satisfying relationships. A bad relationship can be destructive to one or both parties. Relationships fail for three reasons; unresolved hurts (Chapter 4.2), ineffective communication (Chapter 5.6), and not giving and receiving love according to each person's needs (Chapter 7.2). Most relationship problems start when a couple finds there is a "communication problem". How is your relationship? Is it running smoothly using effective communication or do you simply talk at each other, not with each other? Are you just housemates? What are your relationships like with colleagues at work?

Actively listening to what is being said to you and communicating effectively your response, becomes critically important for building and maintaining relationships. Active listening is about using your two ears and one mouth in those exact proportions. Using our X-Y-Z effect communication framework (Chapter 5.5) you will learn to own your emotion, use 'I' language to describe how you feel, and reflect back what someone else has said to show that you have been really listening. Active listening skills are essential for resolving resentments.

The communication model reveals that what you say isn't necessarily what the other person hears. There are plenty of places where "interference" results in something entirely different being heard—or not heard at all! Sometimes the sender of the communication is not expecting you, the listener, to do anything except understand and you may fail to listen long enough, or with sufficient understanding of the sender's feelings, to really understand the definition of the problem.

We are communicating with each other all of the time, both verbally and non-verbally. Research tells us that only 8% to10% of all human communication is verbal, meaning 90% of our communication is non-verbal—what you say is not as important as how you say it. Recall from Chapter 2 that Susan said to Paul, "Paul, it's not what you say, it's how you say it!" In getting his message across, Paul needs to listen carefully, talk clearly, have good eye contact, watch his tone and body language, and use words that match what's being said to him. Using these skills Paul indicates to Susan he has understood what she has said to him, so that his message in reply is not confusing.

Men and women are different—we often don't understand each other. We have learned so far that because of our differing emotional style (Chapter 2), men and women frequently use different ways to release negative energy. In this chapter, we'll explore the communication differences between men and women so we understand each other better and review some differences in cross-cultural communication.

As ineffective communication is a major cause of relationships failing, good communication ensures the receiver gives the sender feedback about what was said, in case there is need for clarification. Let's begin to practise effective communication techniques and build sound communication habits.

5.2 Active Listening

Listening is the essence of any verbal communication—and the reason we were given two ears and only one mouth! Active listening is conveying acceptance, trust and respect at a relationship level. By accepting another's feelings you are saying, "I understand that you feel such-and-such about a particular topic." Active listening encourages openness and a willingness to become engaged with a person. When you are recognized as an active listener you will find that people feel comfortable with you—they will bring their problems to you.

Active listening is particularly helpful if the listener can reflect back to the speaker an understanding of the feelings of what the speaker was going through, as well as just the facts of the event. Sometimes the speaker expresses only the facts. For example, "When the cyclone came through, the roar of the wind was deafening, and it ripped off our roof." A good listener may reply, "You sound like you were pretty scared when you heard the roar of the wind, and when the roof came off, that would have been terrifying." This shows that the listener was able to interpret the emotions of the events that were being described. If he got the feelings correct, even though the speaker did not name the emotions himself, he will feel validated about his experience. He may subsequently use those words (scared, terrified) when recounting the story on another occasion.

The basis of much ineffective listening is two-fold: (1) Failure to distinguish those times when the sender is not expecting you to do anything except understand; and (2) Failure to listen long enough or with sufficient understanding of the sender's feelings to really understand the definition of the problem.

Here are eight typical ways that most people respond in a listening situation that communicate to the sender that it's not acceptable for him or her to have his or her feeling:

1. Ordering, Demanding. "You must try…",
   "You have to stop… "
   (ie, Don't have that feeling, have some other feeling.)

2. Warning, Threatening: "You had better…",
   "If you don't , then…'
   (ie, You'd better not have that feeling.)

3. Admonishing, Moralising: "You should…",
   "It's not nice to … "
   (ie, You're bad if you have that feeling.)

4. Persuading, Arguing, Lecturing;: "Do you realise ...?", "The facts are..."
   (ie, Here are some facts so you won't have that feeling.)

5. Advising, Giving Answers: "Why don't you...?", "Let me suggest..."
   (ie, Here's a solution so you won't have that feeling.)

6. Criticising, Blaming, and Disagreeing: "You aren't thinking about this properly..."
   (ie, You're wrong if you have that feeling.)

7. Praising, Agreeing. "But you've done such a good job... ", "I approve of..."
   (ie, Your feeling is subject to my approval.)

8. Reassuring, Sympathising: "Don't worry...", You'll feel better..."
   (ie, You don't need to have that feeling.)

When the sender perceives that he is getting one of these messages there is a risk that he will become defensive and either justify the feeling further, or close off entirely, never allowing the listener to hear anything deeper than the presenting problem.

An alternative to the above kinds of responses is to acknowledge the other person's feeling by telling them what you understood them to be feeling and thinking. In active listening, the listener summarises in his own words, the content and feeling of the sender's message and states this to the sender to confirm understanding. He or she puts aside his or her own frame of reference and looks at the world from the sender's perspective.

Before we learn how to practise this using effective communication, let's understand the Communication Model and Helping Model of Communication Skills

5.3 Communication Model

Whenever there is communication between two people, one person is the sender of the message and one person is the receiver. The sender first has to encode a message, then send the message—usually in words. At this point they also use non-verbal communication. The receiver picks up both the verbal and non-verbal components of the message and decodes them. There are three areas where interference of the communication process can occur, often resulting in an inaccurate decoding of the message.

These are illustrated in the Communication Model fi below:

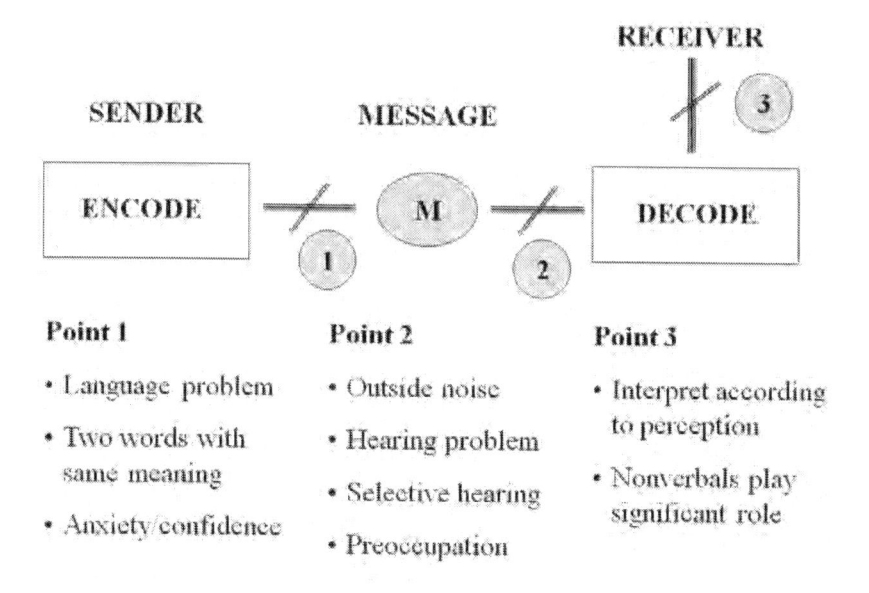

```
         SENDER           MESSAGE           RECEIVER
                                               ╳ ③
         ┌────────┐         ╳                ┌────────┐
         │ ENCODE │ ─── ╳ ─── ( M ) ─── ╳ ─── │ DECODE │
         └────────┘         ①         ②     └────────┘
```

Point 1
- Language problem
- Two words with same meaning
- Anxiety/confidence

Point 2
- Outside noise
- Hearing problem
- Selective hearing
- Preoccupation

Point 3
- Interpret according to perception
- Nonverbals play significant role

At **Point 1** some of the inaccuracy of the communication process can occur through;

1. People speaking a different language,

2. Two words having the same meaning. For example, Mozart's Place or Mozart's birthplace, and

3. The sender experiencing anxiety, so that he doesn't complete sentences but only expresses half-sentences.

At **Point 2** interference of the communication process can occur through;

1. Outside noise affecting what is heard,
2. A genuine hearing problem,
3. Selective hearing. For example, when a person "tunes out" when the topic is not of interest to them, or
4. The receiver is preoccupied with something. For example, a person's attention may be diverted by the television. This can mean that words are heard inaccurately.

At **Point 3** even if the words are heard accurately, the receiver interprets those words according to his or her perception of their meaning. Thoughts in his or her head are often defensive if his or her perception of the message is construed as an order or attack. It is at Point 3 that the nonverbal actions of the sender play a big part in the interpretation. If their tone sounds sarcastic or irritated, if their voice is raised, if their hand gestures, or eye contact are not congruent with the words spoken, the nonverbal messages can have greater impact.

Research suggests that 8 to 12 percent of communication received is through verbal means, and up to 90 percent through nonverbal means. If a wife sarcastically says, "I'm fine," the husband knows that is certainly not the case. To be involved in effective communication, all parties need to be able to clearly construct (encode) their verbal messages. Most importantly, they need to listen, to make sure that what was sent is being received.

5.4 Helping Model of Communication Skills

The Helping Model of Communication Skills can assist you in becoming familiar with skills used by counselors. You can use these skills when called upon to communicate better with a partner, family member, or work colleague in your personal and workplace relationships. The nature of emotional distress and psychosocial problems that people experience can make heavy demands on friends, mentors, supervisors, managers, and professional counselors. The model involves using skills of active listening, reflecting content and paraphrasing the senders' words and feelings.

It is important at the outset of any helping session to make sure that you are comfortable and relaxed, as well as mentally prepared. You may need to practise some relaxation techniques and/or breathing exercises before the session, to ensure that you are operating from a sense of balance and well-being. This will assist you in becoming a more empathic and effective listener. The Helping Model is aimed at assisting someone in managing his or her problem. It is not a therapy for solving the person's problem. It is simply a way for you to improve your interpersonal communication, and apply communication skills to assist others you live and work with.

Please note that professional counseling is specialized work carried out by trained and experienced professionals, who are governed by a professional code of ethics that upholds respect for the individual, and a belief in their uniqueness, human capacity for change, and learning potential. Ultimately the individual alone is responsible for changing his or her circumstances. However, to ensure the best care, a counselor works in conjunction with corporate human resource personnel, doctors, psychiatrists, psychologists, and allied health professionals. This ensures that appropriate referral is made to other mental health professionals to best meet the needs of the client. All counseling interviews are conducted in a professional manner where privacy and confidentiality are assured. Disclosure of confidential information may, in some cases, need to be reported to appropriate persons or agencies.

The Helping Model can assist you in developing a set of attitudes and communication skills which will help you, and people you come into contact with every day, to find out what is going on in other's lives—you help them tell their story. The ABC of the Helping Model of communication skills can be summarized as:

1. Active listening—to build a relationship.
2. Boiling down the problem—looking at alternatives.
3. Challenging the person to act—encouraging the person to take some action.

In developing these skills you need to recognize that building a relationship with the person you are communicating with is the foundational basis for promoting growth. If you fail to establish a rapport with the person you are seeking to help, then you are unlikely to be of any meaningful assistance. Most people want to jump to "B" and "C" as it is our natural response to want to "solve" the person's problem and get a result. In "A" you are finding out what the person is saying, thinking, and feeling—establishing their identity. "A" is foundational to the Helping Model—where you focus on the person, not the problem.

To build up trust with the person you are helping, ensure that you;

1. Focus on the person not the problem.
2. Are accepting, not judging the person.
3. Counsel the person and not give advice.

In our first book we provide a detailed seven-part checklist to assist you in developing your basic communication skills to strengthen your own identity and relationships, and enable you to assist people in your place of work, home and community. Of course, should someone require medical or psychological assistance you will help them the most by referring them to their doctor, allied health or counseling professional. The 7-part checklist:

1. Active listening.
2. Continuing responses—attending skills.

3. Reflection of content—listening with understanding.

4. Reflection of feelings—empathy, the key ingredient.

5. Leading responses—An open invitation to talk

6. Clarifying and summarizing.

7. Attitude—warmth, empathy and genuineness.

5.5 X-Y-Z of Effective Communication

Eff e communication is essential for relationships of any nature—interpersonal, workplace, business, or even service relationships. The communication model and skills set out and practised in the earlier sections of this chapter are fundamental to communication of any kind. What makes your communication effective is when you saturate your communication with empathy—your ability to recognise, understand and be sensitive to a person's current emotion and communicate that to the person in a way that is meaningful to them at the time. Your ability to empathise is communicated through the skills of LLV—levelling, listening, and validating—the XYZ of communication (Adapted from Montgomery & Evans 1984, 1995)[13].

Levelling – "Levelling means telling the other person clearly and non-defensively how you feel, or how you think about a particular issue, rather than trying to hide your feelings or misrepresent them."

Listening – "By listening we mean actively trying to hear what the other person *really* says, rather than assuming you know what he is going to say, or listening to yourself, or interrupting." This gives the listener the opportunity to learn what is going on inside the head and heart of the other person talking. In a relationship, this is often the point where an argument starts – the listener perceives he is being criticised or attacked, gets defensive, and retorts with anger.

Validating – "Validating means to accept as true what the other person tells you about her feelings – rather than denying her feelings, or insisting that she feels as you would, or as you think she should."

The X-Y-Z Formula for Effective Communication

Here is the formula for effective communication for you to practise. It is imperative for effective communication that you drop the "YOU" word. Use "I" statements and not "you" statements to disarm your inner voice, affirm yourself and influence others. Use "I" language in the "X-Y-Z" formula to level about feelings and improve communication from inside a relationship. Start your sentences with, "I feel…".

Use either: "I feel **X** when you do **Y** in situation **Z**."

Example: "I feel very frustrated when you bring the car back to me with almost no petrol, just before I have to go out."

Or: "I feel X when you do Y, because the **effect** on me is Z."

Example: "I feel insecure when I see you looking at other women, because I then think that I'm inadequate."

An effective communication framework is:

Brackets ( ) = optional steps I feel / felt ……….

When you ….. (make this specific, observable, and in the positive)

As / because ……….

(It seems / seemed to me ……….) I'd prefer / I'd like ……….

Example: "I feel angry when you use the phone in our office for personal calls, as I can't get my work done. I would prefer you used this phone only for genuinely urgent calls, please."

Example: "I felt really annoyed when you told me that you'd be home at 7pm and then didn't arrive home until 8:30pm because I kept the children up to see you. It seems to me that my scheduling doesn't matter at all. I'd like you to keep to your commitments please, or phone to tell me you've been held up at the office."

Once you have learned and practised the X-Y-Z formula it is important to recognise and understand communication differences between men and women and across cultures.

5.6 Communication Differences between Men And Women

Expressing your thoughts and feelings clearly, by adopting language appropriate to the situation, is vital for building intimacy and trust in relationships. For example, we know that men and women release negative energy in different ways and that cross-cultural communication has its own difficulties, as some English words and not able to be directly translated to other languages—in some cultures, courtesy may be passed on through intonation or tone rather than using words like 'please' and 'thank you'.

Typically, women release negative energy by talking through their experiences. This seemingly incessant need to "chatter" often drives men to despair—they feel exhausted by it and usually "tune out".

Men however, usually resolve issues in their own head— without any discussion with others. Typically, men release negative energy by reactive behaviour; anger—shouting or physical action) or withdrawal—going to play golf, spending time with a friend to discuss things other than feelings or simply not interact with their partner. This behavior can bewilder women—who generally have a need for quality conversation—and leaves them feeling not listened to, ignored, and even insignificant.

Take a moment to reflect on the behaviors used by men or women that you have experienced, which left you feeling exhausted or unheard.

Did you know that the hippocampus in the woman is more than twice the size of that in the man? The hippocampus, an area in the brain, stores memory to which an emotion is attached. It is a known fact that the woman's larger hippocampus will remember more things that have an emotion attached to it. When it comes to feeling, women have a greater capacity to feel their emotions than men. A woman is more 'hard-wired' to feel the emotion that somebody else may be feeling—to be able to put herself into somebody's shoes—and to communicate that feeling; she has a greater ability to empathize than a man.

We stated earlier, that most relationship problems start when a couple fi there is a "communication problem". The reason there are many problems in relationships is that we just don't understand each other. Men, in particular, don't understand what women need to be happy, and women don't know how to communicate their needs in language that men understand. Men need to be understood, just as women do, it's just that to understand men a woman must think like a man, and vice versa.

Men and women must learn from each other if they are to maintain fulfilling relationships.

What Men need to Understand about Women 12

- Communication is the chief coping mechanism for a woman.
- Women use conversations to understand their relationships.
- Women communicate to discover the range of feelings within themselves.
- Women cope with stress through sharing in nurturing relationships.
- When a woman seeks a partner she is looking for someone to protect her emotional security which allows her the freedom to express her truer self.

- When a woman is upset she needs to talk to sort out how she feels and is not demanding agreement.
- Women have a primary need to be heard.
- Women ask questions and make statements as a plea for men to hear her out and have what concerns her explored.
- Women feel better and more nurtured when men share in her understanding of a situation without necessarily agreeing with her assessment.
- When a woman feels the right to be upset, the less upset she will be.
- When a woman has a chance to share her feelings with the person with whom she is presently upset, she feels more loving and is able to recover more quickly.
- When a woman expresses her feelings she is processing and discovering; seeking information. Feelings are not facts for a woman.
- Women tend to shut down and "give up" communicating if they consistently have no success in being heard.
- Women assume men need what they need.
- WOMEN typically enter into a relationship through communication and emotional stability—wanting a caring, loyal, and understanding partner. Women will only seek sexual fulfillment once emotional intimacy and trust has been established.

What Women need to Understand about Men

- A man's coping strategy is to sort out his thoughts, clarify his priorities, then develop a plan of action, all of which are done without necessarily speaking a word.

- When a man can put his feelings into action (find a solution) he feels more in control of his life.
- Men cope through problem solving and implementing/offering solutions.
- When a man seeks an intimate partner, he wants to be appreciated and needed.
- When a man talks with someone with whom he is upset, his general goal is to get the listener to agree with him so the problem can be corrected.
- Men use communication as a means to pass along information or solve a problem.
- Men feel challenged, threatened even, when questioned.
- Men think an emotional woman is inflexible, has reached a conclusion, and is expressing opinions.
- Men communicate only after determining what they have discovered.
- When a man is upset and talks with a person who upset him, he will remain upset until that person agrees with him. Simply listening to him and nodding sympathetically is not enough if a man is upset.
- When a man expresses his feelings it is more like a fact, something he believes to be true.
- Men assume women need what they need.
- Some men who are feeling hurt in their relationship may find that their desire for sex with their partner diminishes.
- MEN typically enter into a relationship as provider and protector—wanting a supportive and understanding partner. Men seek sexual fulfillment in order to establish and secure emotional intimacy and trust.

Next, a case study...

- **Case Study—Ineffective Communication**

  Situation: A couple once came to see Susan for counseling. The wife was very upset because they were about to move house and the husband had got very cross with her and said, "You can do all of the moving of the house by yourself. I'm sick of you always changing your mind." And so, she dragged him along to counseling and this was the story.

  Two weeks prior to the house move she had said to him, "I'd like to change the covers on the sofa." He had thought to himself, "Well that's a bit of a strange time to want to change the covers on the sofa because we're going to be moving house soon." But he didn't say anything.

  She went on and said, "And I'd like to have a fresh start when we move to our new house. So I'd like the sofa covers to be different." He had his own thoughts about it but he said, "Whatever." She took this to mean "Go ahead". So she spent the next week—which, if you recall, was the week before they moved house—going and having a look at fabrics, talking to girlfriends about it, going on shopping sprees, comparing prices, looking at what was on sale.

  The girlfriends were putting some input in saying, "Look, you're moving house soon and maybe the covers will get dirty when you move. Maybe it's best to move in and see what the décor of the new house is before you purchase. Maybe the kids will jump all over the place or the workmen might make the new covers greasy. Why don't you wait?" After she had received all this input from her girlfriends she thought—"Good Idea! I'll wait".

  So, a couple of nights before this particular counseling session—which was a week later—she went to her husband

and said, "I've decided not to get the sofa covers." She was expecting him to be thrilled—saving money and keeping him informed about what she's thinking—but instead he exploded in a rage. He said, "I'm sick of the way you always change your mind! First of all you want sofa covers, now you don't want sofa covers. First of all you want this house and then you want that house! And then you want those workmen to come and do the moving—you want these movers and then you say you want those movers. I'm sick to death of you always changing your mind!" "Chances are", he continued, "this is going to go on right through the house move. So as far as I'm concerned, you do it all yourself. I'm out. You can look after the whole house move."

And that's what had caused her distress—she was completely taken aback by his reaction. She said it was over the top—and it was over the top. But he was actually expressing his complete despair at what he saw as her always changing her mind.

Work Done In Counseling: When they came to the counseling session and Susan went through the experience with them, the wife said to Susan, "I'm the one who went out and had a look at the sofa covers and I made the decision not to buy them. I thought he'd be very happy because he's a bit worried about the money. I thought it was a good decision and I was just keeping him informed." And, she said, "He doesn't pay any attention to what we do in the house anyway. He's never interested in the décor or the furniture." He protested and said, "That's not true. I am interested." And she said, "When are you interested?" He said, "I'm very interested in the fabrics and the cushions and the curtains, but you never let me have a say." She said, "But you're not interested at all". So then they had this other battle about him allegedly never being interested in anything to do in the house.

Susan stopped them and said to him, "Tell me. What would you have said or thought when your wife came to you and asked about the sofa covers." He said, "She came and asked me about the sofa covers and I thought, what a crazy idea, we're moving house in two weeks. It's going to cost money. They might get dirty. We don't know what the décor's like in the new house. So why are we doing this?"

He had thought about everything that the girlfriends had said. He said to Susan, "I thought all of those things and then I thought, there's no point in getting new sofa covers now, but there is no point telling her because she wants her own way anyway. And that's why I said, 'Whatever.'"

Susan's Advice For Moving Forward: This is what happens so often with ineffective communication. The man thinks all of those options but never says a word. "I had no idea that he thought all those things", said the wife. And he then said to her in the counseling session, "And that's the reason I never say anything about the fabrics or the cushions or what the children wear. Because you want your own way anyway."

This is an example of the way that men and women do things differently. A man's coping mechanism is to sort through his thoughts, clarify his priorities, develop a plan of action and implement it—usually without ever saying a word to anyone else. After all, "we men" are the "providers" and "fie know what to do and don't need anyone telling us to the contrary!

On the other hand, a woman will sort out her thoughts, prioritise, develop strategies for action (the same as a man), but then consult with everyone else before implementing her plan. Men think this constant "chattering" by women with each other is because they can't make up their minds, or are always changing their minds, about things and so need to ask everyone. But this generally is not the case.

It's more in keeping with the nature of a woman to want to discuss and share her thoughts with others; something men find irritating and are not prone to do.

- **Case Study—Communication Differences In A Cross-Cultural Relationship**

An Australian husband and his Belgian wife attended for marriage counseling, at the husband's request. He stated that she was always yelling at him, and he hated it. She said she was fed up with having to raise their three children "on her own", as her husband was frequently distracted with his work.

He complained in session that he "switched" off from helping her as he disagreed with her strict way of dealing with the children. The wife was shocked at her husband's disclosure and asked for more information. He felt safe enough in session to say that he thought his wife was rude and he was appalled, for example, at her lack of manners at the meal table, and how she was raising the children. Susan noted that he had never previously expressed any of this to his wife!

Again the wife asked for specific examples, as she was horrified and defensive at his accusations. He explained, "Well, you never say please or thank you. You just order the children to "pass the butter" or "give me the salt". Again, the wife protested. However, slowly, her defensiveness turned to understanding as she considered his complaints.

She explained to Susan, and her husband, that in her Flemish language, the 'please' and 'thank you' were automatically expressed as an inflection in the request or the demand. She was able to realize that when she translated directly to English, the inflection was lost, and so were the courteous *magic word*s, 'please' and 'thank you'. She then herself became upset at the years she had been speaking to her children like this—when she spoke to them in English.

Fortunately, the children were bilingual as she also spoke to them in Flemish. She asked her husband to help her in rectifying this, and in pointing out to her when this happened. Had the husband not been so avoidant, this problem could have been rectified a lot earlier. Her husband showed compassion at the obvious misunderstanding that had been driving a wedge between them, and he was able to grasp that his silence and withdrawal had been driving her anger and frustration at him. The couple were able to salvage their relationship.

In cross-cultural relationships, the receiver does not always correctly interpret what the sender intends.

If men knew that women, as a general rule, like to communicate and like to talk about their feelings, one of the greatest gifts he would give his female partner would be to say, "Would you like to talk? Is there anything you're troubled about? Is there anything that annoys you?" And then give her the gift of time to let her offload.

From a man's perspective, he will need you to tell him the facts and not expect him to understand feelings. Expectations and wrong communication can cause a great deal of resentment. Men need clear directions, so women (who can be very indirect) need to understand that men don't always pick up the nuances of an indirect reply, and need clear instructions.

You can learn more of the differences between men and women and unmet expectations in Chapter 7. We want now to turn to how each of us can manage the emotions of others.

6
Manage The Emotion of Others — Recognizing, Knowing And Predicting Change

6.1 Introduction

To manage emotions of others, and influence them, you first must be able to manage your own emotions. People high in the skill of managing the emotions of others typically ...

- Are aware of the impact of their mood—they opt out of the emotional see-saw.

- Remain open to what they are feeling—they do not suppress or ruminate on their emotion.

- Challenge their inner voice using the 4-step cognitive framework—they have given up rejecting parts of themselves.

- Have learned to use the "GAP" between event and response giving them a long "fuse" allowing excess adrenalin to be released from their body.

- Can predict emotional change using their ability to recognize emotions, knowledge of emotion chains and blends, and understanding the change process.

Can you manage your own emotion? Are you willing to give up: not owning your feelings and blaming others; explaining and complaining; being oppositional; being angry, irritated and frustrated; with drawing from and avoiding your fear and anxiety? If you can do this, as well as know and understand the change process, distinguish grief from depression, develop knowledge of emotion chains and blends, and are exceptional at empathizing, then you are ready to manage the emotions of others.

6.2 First Manage Your Own Emotions

This is the most important emotional skill of all because it is the most effective way to change "perception". In the long run what you have to do is change your behaviour and the perception of your stakeholders; those whom you want to influence. Between the two, changing perception is the far more challenging assignment. People find it very difficult to change existing judgements, inferences, assumptions, expectations, and beliefs about you. You choose to influence others by following-up on stakeholder feedback and suggestions. Don't rely on past interactions or neglect your new found ease of asking for feedback.

A well-worn definition of lunacy is: "Doing the same thing over and over again and expecting different results." Different results require different actions. The Chinese define risk as the combination of danger and opportunity. Greater risk means you have greater opportunity to do well, but also greater danger of doing badly. You have to be willing to destabilise your own status quo, to move from your comfort zone, in order to reach your desired effect.

The bottom line is: if a belief, value or expectation you hold isn't working, change it.

Emotional arousal creates awareness of your defense against change. How you react when change is placed in front of you will depend upon whether you have an "avoidant" or "reactive" emotional style (Chapter 2). The emotion that is generated in you by change, or the thought of change, will vary from person to person. If you are an "avoidant" person change will create arousal in you that will linger much longer than if you are a "reactive" person. This is true whether the arousal brings a positive feeling, for example, a sense of excitement about a trip overseas; or a negative feeling, such as, anger or anxiety.

Conditioning has you trapped in fixed patterns of thoughts, feelings, and actions. Appraisal of events—people and circumstances—trigger in you automatic responses that have not served you well. You have been programmed into making choices automatically. You are what you are today because of the choices you have made. Choose to sow emotional wealth.

To sow emotional wealth means to have the ability to do the right thing. It means having a mind that so trusts in your emotional skills as its rock that nothing can deflect from your mindset. Being so anchored in your emotional brain's capacity to learn appropriate behavioral responses ensures that nothing can possess you, such as an inner critic wanting to drag you back to your pre-conditioned state.

Emotional wealth is empowering. It's about you giving up conditioning and regaining control over your identity; reframing your memory, current thoughts, and predictions in a way that your appraisal of them produces the 'right' response or reaction you want. Emotional wealth is trusting in your emotions to make no-lose decisions that will serve you and all those with whom you come into contact.

Negative emotions are the stuff of past conditioning—they will raise your stress level and harm you physically and psychologically. Positive emotions, including love, trust, compassion, forgiveness, joy, and hope, are the stuff of present moment awareness. They will reduce your stress and help relax your body to enjoy a life of ease. In sowing emotional wealth you are choosing to give to others in a way that honours their right to be loved, respected, empowered, and treated with dignity. You are living a life for others.

Equipped with your new skill of changing past conditioning you are free to manage the emotions of others. You now have a built in biological mechanism to deflect criticism or judgements and not take things personally. This frees up your energy to manage emotions in others and build your relationships.

6.3 The Change Process

Change is a process, a movement from one state to another. The path mandated in this book is self-directed change for the better, which represents an individual's current life situation. The movement of one ball away from those encased by the hexagon, symbolises self-directed change for good in the future; from what is known and within your comfort zone to values, goals, and dreams of what is possible for you as an individual.

We learned in Chapter 1 that the human body is programmed to perceive change in the internal and external environment and respond to it. We acknowledged that positive change has a non-problem status. Negative change arouses our defence mechanisms—our conditioned response—mediated by the emotional brain. Attachment by many people to defence mechanisms—such as denial, projection or displacement—is the conditioned response based on fear, insecurity, and lack of awareness.

- For example;

    We may <u>deny</u> the existence of external threats.

    <u>E</u>xample: refusing to accept the reality of a life- threatening influence.

    We often <u>project</u> our feelings onto someone else when we feel uncomfortable or embarrassed.

    <u>Example</u>: When we do not arrive at a scheduled interview on time we may say, "I can hear you are really made at me."

    In <u>d</u>isplacement, we choose an inappropriate, rather than an appropriate, expression for an unacceptable arousal (over reaction).

    <u>Example</u>: You may be really angry about your workload, or feel overlooked because something you submitted to your boss has not been considered. So you target the boss; "He is a pig!".

Fear, insecurity and lack of awareness require that we step into reality where emotions are fully experienced in the present and give up these conditioned responses.

Our study of personality, the bio-psycho-physical interactions in the stress response detailed in Chapter 1, our work with more than 4,500 individual clients from 83 nationalities in Australia and Singapore, and our 35 years experience in human support, academia and business, lead us to the following conclusion in the analysis of human identity;

- Avoidant people are prone to experiencing fear- provoking anxiety—leading to flight/withdrawal.

- Reactive people are prone to experiencing memory- driven anger—leading to fight/aggression.

Knowing how people will respond after an emotional event—knowing their emotional style—allows you to predict the change process they will flow through when aroused by negative change, such as loss or grief.

The ten stages of the change process (Figure 6.1) follow what many people experience when they suffer the loss of a loved one through death, insecurity of a job loss, an incapacity through mental illness, physical harm or injury, fear of the onset of old age, loss of regular contact with family and friends through relocation, and children leaving home. With awareness and understanding of the change process you can better manage your own and the emotions of others.

The ten steps of the change process[13] are:

1. Shock/Disbelief – You have been made to withstand pain, trauma and even, great tragedy.

2. Emotional Arousal – Your feelings signal bodily needs. Terrible loss is felt as a surging of feelings within. You feel uncontrollable discomfort.

3. <u>Physical Symptoms</u> – Intense arousal causes physiological responses to occur that affect your ability to sleep, eat or concentrate.

4. <u>Guilt/Self-reproach</u> – You feel a sense of responsibility for the change, and begin to think about what you did or did not do, or what you should have done to prevent it.

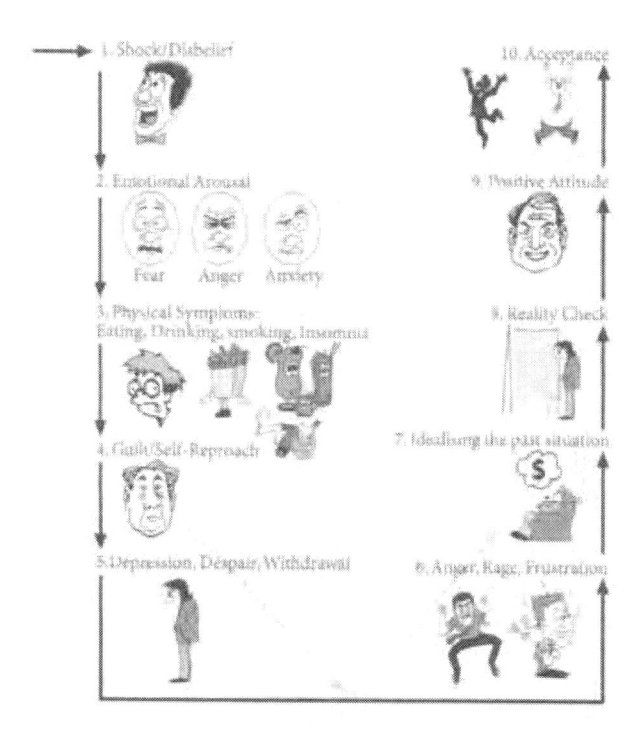

Figure 6.1 The Change Process

5. <u>Depression/Despair/Withdrawal</u> – You are preoccupied about the change and cannot concentrate on anything else. As you have probably not experienced some of these feelings before, you despair that something is happening to your mind. This causes you to withdraw from activities, family and friends, to hide your feelings. At the same time you feel isolated and alone.

6. Anger/Rage/Frustration – Hostility and resentment take over as you have been holding back emotion. You blame "out" – the doctor, your partner, God, often someone who is closest to you.

7. Idealising The Past Situation – You take solace in thinking about how it was in the past.

8. Reality Check – You are beginning to approach acceptance of change. The unreality of your present position slowly begins to dawn on you.

9. Positive Attitude – Mood changes in response to positive thoughts, during growing periods of acceptance.

10. Acceptance – You are now your old self and are stronger emotionally because of your experience of change.

Change may come as a shock and be totally unexpected. Change may be planned for in advance. When the reality of change sets in, people experience the stages within the change process to varying degrees. If you spend too much time in any one of the stages it may be a sign of "dis-ease" in which case you should seek professional help.

- **Case Study—Managing Grief Through Transition Situation:** Dan sought some clarity on some niggling feelings he was having. He had decided to relocate from Adelaide to Melbourne as he had been unable to secure suitable long term work. After two weeks in Melbourne in his new permanent job, he reported that he was feeling, "Kind of lost and sad". Susan told him he was describing grief.

  There were many things Dan was going through as he started his new life in Melbourne. Even though he knew some people, it was still difficult to settle into a new environment, and he felt lost for a while. And it is a different feeling to just visiting a new place— which of course is exciting and wonderful—because you know it is temporary. When you are visiting a new place, you EXPECT to feel lost and not know your way around. And to not know anybody. Moving there permanently is very different.

Susan's Assessment: Grief is that feeling of having lost something of value. Dan felt he had lost many things by moving to Melbourne. His church family, for one. His beloved dog, two. The sense of security that he belonged somewhere, three. Being known by many people in Adelaide, four. Being sought after because he was known by many people, five. Even his little granny flat, six. Mia, his partner, seven. And probably more, like always having someone to visit. Or a camping trip to organize—that was a big one, as Dan had a great group of camping friends who were always off somewhere!

Even though Dan sort of 'knew' Melbourne and had visited, this was different. This move constituted the loss of all those things he listed. And for that, he felt grief—a hollow and empty sort of feeling. Susan reassured him that this feeling would pass, and that in order for it to pass, he actually had to feel the pain of it. It is the brain's way of adjusting to the new situation— decoding that the new environment is no longer a "danger" or threat.

Susan knew one thing about Dan that needed addressing, which was that he always had to be doing something or visiting someone. She understood his need for stimulation, and she knew that Dan hated being bored. She pointed out that for a while now, he would have no one to visit, and that would mean more time on his own. At these times, she told him, he may even feel depressed.

Outcome: Susan wrote to Dan, "Learn to recognise the feeling of ALONE being different to LONELY and that ALONE (read, UNSTIMULATED) can feel BORING.

This is not the same as DEPRESSED but can easily be interpreted as such. It may be the sad feeling you describe— and certainly boring is a down/low feeling— but the moment there is somewhere to go, something to do, the mood changes because the stimulation kicks in."

Susan gave Dan a list of things that he could do during the times when he was alone and wondering what to do with himself—quite apart from considering the wonderful advantages of spending time by himself. She told him he could:

1. Sleep—of which you need heaps, to catch up
2. Listen to music and just enjoy it
3. Watch DVDs and movie downloads – especially those you laugh at
4. Sort photos
5. Start a blog
6. Update your website/Facebook to reflect your changed circumstances
7. Complete your tax return
8. Pay your bills and check if any fines need attention
9. Clean your car
10. Journal your thoughts
11. Read the cards people gave you and reminisce
12. Write an email to someone you think about often but never write to
13. Prepare a budget for this year's income and expenses
14. Wash some clothes and do the ironing
15. Do some leatherwork

16. Research a course you may wish to do

17. Ring someone you know in Melbourne just for the hell of it

18. Do some exercise, such as, take a long walk, swim or bike ride

19. Make a cup of tea and think of the people you love the most while you drink it

Susan advised Dan: "Also know that on occasions you will cry for no particular reason, you just will. And those tears are good because they contain a chemical that balms the body and soothes the soul. And after a good cry (Note we never say, a really bad cry), you will sleep well and then tomorrow is a new day."

Susan told Dan that she had been remembering how it was when she was in Germany in 1972, away from home and English speakers for such a long time. No mobiles and computers in those days. "My goodness I had some lonely times. On two occasions that I recall vividly, I was suicidal, and had a passing thought of jumping under a tram as it approached. Then my sane mind took over and I realised this lonely feeling was a passing one, and that as soon as I was back with people who spoke my language I would be OK. Those experiences led me into Social Work and counseling, I must tell you, as I wanted to always be able to help someone who needed to talk and had no one to talk to—even if they could not speak English."

Susan's Advice For Moving Forward: Susan pointed out to Dan that he had had many changes in his 22 years, and had adjusted and adapted amazingly. Going to college as a boarder in 2006 was one of his most difficult transitions and this one to Melbourne was about the same intensity. She congratulated him on being successful in taking the new permanent job, and reminded him that he would soon able to repay some debts and get himself on a sound financial footing.

Susan reminded Dan he may wonder at times if his move to Melbourne was the right decision. Susan told him we never intentionally make wrong decisions. We make the best decision we can with the information available to us at the time, and from time to time the decision has to be reviewed in light of new information. For now, he should know that Melbourne has more to offer him in his chosen industry, and that one day soon he may be glad he made the move.

Let's now distinguish grief from depression and recognise why this is important.

6.4 Distinguish Grief from Depression

For several weeks and months after the death of a loved one, you may experience the emotional pain of his or her passing. You will feel the grief and loss intensely, and maybe also relief that your loved one can now be still and at peace, perhaps after a serious illness.

There is no easy way around grief, no set pattern. Each of you will experience different emotions as you remember the person who died and what he or she meant in your life. Perhaps you will feel shock at the death, extreme sadness, numbness, or an overwhelming sense of loss of his or her vitality and love of life. Some of you will cry a lot. Some of you will express disbelief that the person has gone. Others may be feeling a little queasy in your stomach, maybe anxious about your own health even. In your grief and sadness you will all pass through the change process and experience all or some of the normal grief reactions.

Figure 6.2—Normal Grief Reactions

FEELINGS	PHYSICAL SENSATIONS
Sadness, Anger, Fear, Resentful Guilt and Self-reproach	Hollowness, feel sick in the stomach, nausea
Anxiety, Overwhelming loss Loneliness (Isolation) Fatigue,	Tightness in the chest and in the throat Over sensitivity to noise, headaches A sense of depersonalization (out of body)
Disbelief, Helplessness, Life is empty	Breathlessness, panic attacks, weakness in the muscles, high blood pressure
Shock, Yearning, Indifference	Lack of energy ("can't be bothered"), lethargic
Emancipation Relief, Numbness	Dry mouth, more susceptible to illness

COGNITIONS	BEHAVIOURS
Disbelief, Preoccupation, Confusion,	Sleep disturbances, Appetite disturbances
Sense of presence, How will I cope?	Absent-minded behavior, Social withdrawal
Hallucinations, Suicidal thoughts	Dreams of the deceased, Avoiding reminders
Why? What will people say?	
Why didn't he say something?	Searching, calling out, Sighing, Restless over activity
Nothing in my life will be perfect again	Crying, Treasuring objects, Carrying objects
	Can't concentrate

Understanding normal grief reactions prepares you to better manage emotions of others. Two primary ingredients in grief are (1) the experience of loss (including anticipated loss), and emotional pain. Depression and grief are different, although they may manifest similar characteristics (sleep disturbance, appetite disturbance, and intense sadness). In a grief reaction there is not the loss of self-esteem commonly found in most clinical depressions. That is, people who have lost someone do not regard themselves less because of such loss or if they do, it tends to be only for a brief time.

- **Case Study—Grief versus Depression**

  Situation: Marcia, a single woman in her 20's, was referred for counseling by her doctor, to whom she had gone with feelings of depression. She had recently travelled interstate to attend the funeral of an old boyfriend who had died tragically, and his family had contacted her to advise of his death. Since returning home from the funeral, Marcia described that there had been "lots of crying, lots of sadness, and not much of getting on with things".

  Marcia also described feeling isolated and alone, and believed that nobody understood her or her feelings.

  In fact, she herself did not understand her feelings - she had, after all, broken up with this boyfriend two years earlier, and got on with her life since then, so why these strange reactions to his death and funeral?

  She was unable to understand why she was having such mood swings, doing well one day and the next, spending almost the entire day weeping. She felt the need to talk to someone, yet did not want to burden her new friends with talk of an old boyfriend in another state who had recently died.

  Susan's Assessment: Susan helped Marcia identify that this was indeed the first death that she had experienced of a significant person in her life. Susan described normal grief reactions, and Marcia agreed that the feelings of grief were new to her. Whilst she was no longer in a relationship with her old boyfriend, he had for some years been a very important person to her, and his death had resurrected feelings of closeness they had shared and lost when they broke up (now lost forever), in addition to the loss of plans and dreams they had once had for the future.

Work Done In Counseling: The death of someone young usually brings the response, "what a waste of a life", particularly if the person has (or has had) a place of importance in your life. This is a reflection that you believe that the person had a contribution to make to life, and that this contribution will now never be realized. Susan also explained to Marcia that seeing the young man's family again at the funeral, a family in which she was quite involved for some years, also brought about feelings of loss. Marcia was then able to recognize that she was grieving the loss of many things that had been signify to her and not just the death of her old boyfriend. She discussed with Susan whether she had perhaps moved state (to another job) and 'moved on' so quickly after the breakup, that she had not adequately grieved the loss of the relationship. Until now.

With any loss comes reactions of grief, and Susan normalized Marcia's responses by providing an information sheet outlining the common reactions to grief, some of which include feelings of guilt, yearning that things could have been diff self-reproach, intense sadness, and a myriad of physical symptoms, such as appetite disturbance, sleep disturbance, muscle aches, headache, unexplained pains, fatigue, and a preoccupation with the death (loss event). A person may also feel hollow in the stomach, and withdraw from social contact, whilst at the same time feel very lonely.

Outcome: Marcia benefited from the counseling session. Once she had "told her story" and Susan had advised her that her feelings were normal for the situation (it was the situation that was abnormal), she was able to recognise that the feelings she had were appropriate for the shock and grief she had endured. She no longer felt anxious that she was "cracking up". She identified that she had a supportive family and friends and a satisfying job, and that these afforded her a personal security and sense of well-being.

Marcia continued to manage her own life well, which she had always done, after just one counseling session. Within one month, Marcia was successful in providing practical and emotional support to a friend of a friend, a woman in her 20's, who was grieving the death of her boyfriend in a car accident. Marcia was by now so familiar with normal grief reactions, that she was able to help someone else.

Susan's Advice For Moving Forward: Grief is an extremely unique and painful experience, which a person feels in their entire body, not just in their mind. There are a number of physical and psychological reactions that are considered normal for grief, and knowing them can be reassuring that you are not "losing the plot"! Grief can last for weeks or months, sometimes longer, and is often misdiagnosed as depression if the person fails to tell the doctor or counsellor of a significant loss.

Grief and depression are different, even though they manifest some similar characteristics, such as intense sadness, appetite disturbance and sleep disturbance. The difference is that with grief, a person is unlikely to suffer a loss of self esteem, and if they do, it is only for a short period of time.

A person knows that their grief is resolving if they recognize periods of time throughout the day when they are not feeling the pain. But once they do think about their loss, the pain returns like a big wave. With the pain comes sadness, weeping and a constant thinking of the loss. As time passes (months), the person starts to have more pain-free times than pain episodes, and they are able to have moments of enjoyment and even laughter and feelings of normality, in between the waves of grief. All this is normal, and is part of the process of grief.

Grief needs to be experienced fully, pain and all, for it to eventually resolve. People who deny their grief, and try hard not to hurt, will eventually experience a pathological grief, with complex and confusing painful symptoms. Fun and laughter seem taboo, as if you are being disloyal to the one who has died. Grief is resolved when you can think of the person or thing you have lost, but not have a physical reaction to that picture in your mind.

Often after a change, such as loss of a loved one, a change of job, moving house, relocation to another country, people experience feelings of loss, but don't recognize it as such. They will often wonder if they are depressed due to feelings of sadness and changes to sleeping and eating patterns. Usually this is related to grief, not depression. Once a person has experienced the pain of grief they will say that it gives them a better understanding of what others are going through after a significant loss.

6.5 Develop Emotional Knowledge

Developing emotional knowledge is crucial to managing the emotion of others. Emotional information can be learned; you are not stuck with what you were born with or have been conditioned with to date. Emotions combine and progress and change in intensity through individual and relationship transitions. Being able to label emotions and understand their different combinations, of emotion chains and emotion blends, is important in developing your personal awareness and in your dealings with other people.

Emotion Chain

An emotion chain describes when several emotions are experienced in succession as a response to an event. When you experience an emotion chain following an event, such as the death of a loved one or being retrenched, you are likely to experience a sequence of distinct and reasonably predictable emotions that progress over time. Understanding emotion chains provides the ability to manage each emotion as they arise because they are recognized as normal for the event. This is an emotional skill used by counselors and psychologists and can be learned by everyone.

People skilled in understanding emotion chains are able to;

- predict how people's emotions will change over time
- anticipate people's responses and don't get caught off-guard
- communicate and connect with people on a deep emotional level.

Three examples of emotional "chains";

- The death of a loved one can lead to sadness, grief, anger, guilt, and depression.
- Drinking alcohol can cause you to feel distrustful, angry, and disgusted with yourself.
- Getting a lead part in a play can make you excited, pride, surprise, amazed, thrilled

Emotion Blend

Understanding emotion blends is your ability to analyse blends of emotions into their parts and conversely, to assemble simple feelings together into compound emotions (blend). If you are a reactive person it is likely that a low level of annoyance will combine with irritation to build into high intensity rage—often displayed as inappropriate behaviour. The complex emotion we label contentment is comprised of feelings of security, happiness and relief. When experienced by an avoidant person, contentment will promote a rapid depletion of built- up adrenalin (stress) from the body.

People skilled in their understanding of emotion blends;

- know emotions as a resource and are spot-on in figuring people out
- quickly adjust to new situations
- don't get confused by mixed and contradictory emotions.

Examples of emotion blends;

- Concern—anxiety, caring and anticipation
- Contentment—security, happiness, relief
- Appreciation—love, gratitude, warmth
- Confident—pride, lucky, accepted
- Despair—insecure, anxious, helpless

How can you know that another person is describing the same experience you describe using the same emotional language? You can't. However, more intense forms of emotion state are distinctive. When you have developed knowledge of emotion chains and emotion blends, and can correctly perceive how another person processes emotion—either as an avoidant or reactive person—you can use these abilities to enhance your thinking or cognitive ability. This ability places you in the enviable position of being an effective "agent of change" to help others improve their emotional awareness.

Being able to predict emotion chains and recognize blends of emotion will assist you to empathize accurately with others; thus ensuring they are helped by your understanding of their emotional pain.

6.6 Be Exceptional at Empathizing

Actors must be properly inspired to act their part. A good actor can transport himself to experience emotions in an alternate modality—get into another space—rapidly, using his emotional imagination. He in fact can "fl

depending upon what part he is called on to play and feel an emotion that is authentic, that is, the emotion is felt rather than intellectualized.

Like an actor, there will be times when you are called upon to display some acting skills in order to guide, direct, and influence the behaviour or actions of others. There will be times when you will be cast into a role that is vitally important to your success and the success of others. You will be required to use your emotional imagination to "flick-the-switch", generating the emotion of others and feeling it so that the feeling is authentic and natural. For example, you will be able to feel "disappointment" versus describing what "disappointment" is.

The ability to generate sensations at the appropriate level of intensity (empathy) is crucial to managing the emotions of others. Egan[14] (1998) wrote, "Although many people may feel 'empathy' for others, the truth is that few know how to put it into words. Empathy, as a communication of understanding of the other, remains an improbable event in everyday life."

Basic empathy is the communication to another person of your understanding of his or her point of view with respect to his or her experiences, behaviors, and feelings.[15] Basic empathy involves translating your understanding of a person's experiences, behaviors and feelings into a response that shares that understanding with that person.

The truth is, most people cannot empathize. Our effective communication framework (Chapter 5) lets the other person know that you have recognized and understood his or her emotional displays and behaviors. Additionally, active listening skills (Chapter 5) and verbal and non-verbal acknowledgement of others' emotions, or a combination of both, are excellent techniques for validating the emotions of others.

Here is a formula for expressing empathy:

You feel... [here name the correct emotion expressed by the client/customer/peer/boss/ direct report and some indication of its intensity]

Because (or when)... [here indicate the key experiences and/or behaviors that give rise to the emotion]

- Example:

    A woman in a self-help group is talking about a relationship with a man. She says:

    "About a couple of months ago he began being abusive, calling me names, describing my defects. To tell you the truth, that's why I joined this group, but I haven't had the courage to talk about it till now. The couple of times I've tried to stand up for myself, he became even more abusive. He hasn't hit me or anything, but… So I've been just taking it, just sitting there and taking it… like a dog or something. Do you think that this is just his bizarre way of getting rid of me? Why doesn't he just tell me?"

    Key experience(s): being abused by companion, escalation in abuse

    Key behavior(s): trying to stand up for herself, becoming passive, trying to figure out if this is his way of getting rid of her.

    Key feelings/emotions: distraught, confused, angry

    Empathic response (using formula): "You **feel** angry and confused **because** the abuse came from out of the blue. You're wondering whether this is just his way of ending the relationship."

We have been on a journey to emotional health. You now recognize the impact of stress on your body; have explored your emotional style, learned how you generate emotion and manage pain, developed communication skills and discovered how you can manage the emotion of others. These are necessary steps in a process that helps you manage your responses after emotional events in your life.

Why have you been interested to read this book so far? We hope it is because you want to use your new found emotional skills to reconnect—get your relationships back on track. In the next chapter of we provide you strategies to achieve this goal.

7

Reconnect And Reduce Your Stress — Get Your Relationships Back On Track

7.1 Introduction

Relax Release Let Go is about learning and applying skills to manage your emotional responses in various situations and guide your thinking and actions to lead a more meaningful life.

The subtitle of this book—How to reduce stress after an emotional event—reminds us that emotion impact is everything we do. Why is this important? Because everything in life is about what you feel. You feel exhilarated on securing that new job, overjoyed on the birth of your child, frustrated when you don't get your own way, anxious while you await exam results.

What you feel about you partner or children determines how you relate to them. What you feel about your boss—Is he consistent and approachable or narcissistic and a pig?—will affect your productivity and stress level at work. What you feel about yourself—your esteem—determines if you have got your inner voice in check and whether or not you are happy, fulfilled and successful in your life.

We have pointed out in this book that positive emotion has a non-problem status. On the other hand, negative emotion (stress) arises because of your inappropriate cognitive appraisal of a situation—what you think about an event. Often what you feel in your body is automatic—the conditioned response. We have argued that each event is an opportunity for change—from a negative emotion to a positive emotion. How you manage negative emotion after an event—how you manage your appraisal—is therefore critical to your physical, emotional and psychological health and ultimately, your relationships and financial health.

Emotion management is critical to your financial health. When you are emotionally constipated you are more likely to underperform in your employment, professional or business activities, and could suffer substantial financial loss. We have anecdotal evidence from former coaching and counseling clients that this is, in fact, the case. We have also received feedback from clients who say they have experienced substantial increase in their income after applying the techniques in this book.

Emotions impact social behaviors. If you have not realised it until now, how you manage your own emotions and the emotions of others is reflected in the relationships you have constructed in your life to date. How are your relationships working out for you? Have your conditioned responses impacted favourably or unfavourably on other people? Have your behaviors resulted in sound trusting relationships? Are you connected or disengaged? Are you experiencing a failed relationship at home, at work or in your community? If so, how has this breakdown in your relationships impacted on your health and on the health of those you love? What are your emotions telling you? Are you able to;

- "Flick-the-switch" and change your mood to fit a situation? For example, if you arrive at work angry at your spouse, how does that feeling alter what you see or do on the job? How might fear influence your financial decisions about a new project being considered? If you are feeling depressed, how will you contribute effectively to a meeting about marketing or sales projections? Are your social relationships governed by compassion and gratitude or feelings of insecurity, entitlement and grandeur?

- Create environments in the workplace that make people feel more optimistic and positive by communicating and interacting in ways that motivate and engage others?

- Help others see things from different range of perspectives and assist them to identify more effective ways of responding (behaving) to events that are causing them adversity—are you an active listener?
- Demonstrate an understanding of and communicate to others what they are feeling – can you empathize with others?

This book has been about helping you make lasting change in your own behavior and the behavior of others to build, and in some cases salvage, effective long-term positive relationships— to reconnect. We have challenged you to recognize that you are today what you have chosen to be and suggested ways in which you can manage *change* through self-management and social management, so you can enjoy a more meaningful life.

This final chapter includes strategies for getting your relationships back on track. We will show you how to handle indifference, unmet expectations, and difficult people. We tell you the secret of what makes an intimate relationship special— how to give love according to how your partner receives love. This secret alone has helped salvage many relationships. Finally, we explain how to build your sandcastle of trust and feel secure in your relationships. Let's begin by exploring the relationship cycle.

7.2 Relationship Cycle

One place where most people experience change is in their close personal and family relationships. We proposed in Chapter 5.1 that relationships fail for three major reasons; (1) unresolved hurts, (2) ineffective communication, and (3) each person in the relationship not knowing how to give and receive love to meet the needs of the other person.

The relationship cycle[16] (figure 7.1) describes the four major components of a relationship; effective communication, emotional intimacy, sensuality, and sexuality. In Chapter 5.6 we described how;

Women typically enter into a relationship through communication and emotional stability—wanting a caring, loyal, and understanding partner. Women will only seek sexual fulfillment once emotional intimacy and trust has been established.

Men typically enter into a relationship as provider and protector—wanting a supportive and understanding partner. Men seek sexual fulfillment in order to establish and secure emotional intimacy and trust.

Whilst this is not true for all men and women, it does highlight a major difference between the genders that is the cause for some relationship breakdowns. Men need to understand how women operate, and women need to understand how men operate. Additionally, men are typically not effective communicators in relationships—but they can learn to be.

Figure 7.1

Relationship Cycle*

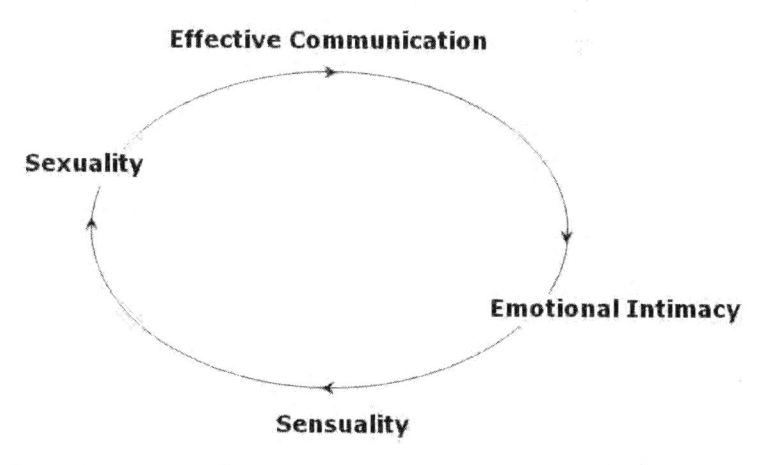

Effective Communication

Sexuality

Emotional Intimacy

Sensuality

* Adapted from "Continuum of bonding behaviours" – Dr Rosie King (1997) Good Loving, Great Sex, Random House, Sydney, p. 228.

There are four diff levels of intimacy to be experienced within the continuum of the relationship cycle. Whilst it is more directed toward intimate sexual relationships and bonding behaviors, there are two aspects of the relationship cycle—communication and intimacy— which are crucial for building effective relationships in your family, work place and community.

1. **Effective communication**—is for building relationships in the workplace, at home, and in the community. As you communicate and self-disclose—through leveling, listening, and validating—you honour the other person's right to be heard. Refer back to Chapter 5.5 for a refresher on this topic.

2. **Emotional intimacy**—is a place where people feel safe when discussing issues that are important to a relationship. Emotional intimacy is definitely for close friends, family, and lovers. A degree of emotional intimacy is necessary in some work place environments where people need to share information in an atmosphere of trust—medical practitioners, for example.

3. **Sensuality**—is experienced by people who delight in the senses, and is a non-sexual component of a relationship. It is particularly important for the partner in a relationship who wants to distance himself or herself from sexual contact with the other partner, to express his or her love in this way.

4. **Sexuality**—the final step in intimate relationships, covering a broad range of sexual behaviours.

The relationship cycle is particularly useful in illustrating what areas in a relationship need working on. For example, an avoidant person—male or female—who has been distancing himself or herself due to emotional arousal, will often have a need for quality conversation or time with their partner. It is common that until this need has been met, an avoidant or sensitive person is unlikely to want to participate in sensuality or sexuality.

Sex therapist and educator, Dr Rosie King (1997), writes that couples who fall in love for the first time enjoy a period of limerence for between 12 to 18 months.

> Limerence is a term coined by American psychologist Dorothy Tennov to describe the fabulous feelings most of us experience in the early stages of a romantic relationship.[17]

When limerence is at its peak, all four segments of the relationship cycle may be operating, as the partners experience their love and bond together. As limerence fades and people get tired of being the "perfect partner", little arguments and irritations creep into a relationship and different parts of the relationship cycle will fade. This is exactly the point at which people struggling to keep a relationship alive should begin the difficult task of building or salvaging a secure long term relationship. Sadly, for many couples this does not happen and their relationship begins a downward spiral, often ending in separation and divorce.

The relationship cycle helps you put our partner's needs into perspective. Once you become aware of where you are in the relationship cycle and which issues need addressing—what you are feeling and why you are feeling it—you are on the right path to managing your responses, reconnecting with others, and enjoying a happy and more meaningful life.

- **Q & A—Where Is The Love?**

    QUESTION: *I love my husband and he says he loves me too, but there's no intimacy anymore. We are each other's best friend, we talk and laugh and do things with the children, but there's no sex. We don't even talk about it anymore. There are no arguments, no demands, nothing. Where has the passion gone? I miss it.*

    ANSWER: You're not the only one asking! Many couples find themselves in this situation of no sex for a long period of time.

And they don't know how to "get started" again. It is almost worse than being a teenager again. At least then you had raging hormones on your side and some feelings of novelty.

Many men—like most women—need low levels of conflict to desire sexual intimacy. So examine your communication. Are you often irritable with one another or critical of each other? If you talk about your feelings, does your husband interpret that as complaining or nagging?

Does your husband travel frequently? The lack of intimacy could be because he works long hours, often across several time zones. When we are physically and mentally tired our libido drops. And as some men age, the urge for sex decreases—although their interest doesn't! You may need to let him know you're still interested in him and find him attractive.

Your husband may also feel content and secure in your marriage because of the way you care for him. Perhaps you affirm your love by doing things for him, or giving him gifts. This could mean he feels adequately loved— without physical contact.

But if you miss the physical part of your relationship you must take the risk and tell him. Don't hold back for fear of rejection, he may be doing exactly the same. Rather than making him feel at fault, explain you miss being close to him and suggest ways in which you can spend time together as a couple. Perhaps with improved communication and a feeling of closeness, intimacy will soon follow.

In the remainder of this chapter we provide strategies and techniques to help you work on different aspects of your personal and social relationships—to get them back on track;

- Indifference—Communicate effectively with your partner, so he or she feels listened to, validated and wants to reengage.

- Unmet expectations—Self-manage your emotions, releasing stored hurts.

- Handling difficult people—Conduct social management of the emotions of others, so you don't misinterpret cues and information.

- Giving and receiving love—Practise giving love to meet your partner's felt need for love, which paradoxically, gives you an abundance of his or her love in return.

- Sandcastle of trust—Build relationships that value trust as foundational to social behavior.

7.3 Indifference

Indifference is the ambivalent state of not caring any more. It is more damaging to relationships than resentment, because you lose any passion to make things right.

You simply give up and think, "Whatever!" At least when there is resentment, you still have strong feelings, and yearn for things to be different. You experience anger, which can motivate you to still do things about the relationship. You may still organize events, try to communicate, and attempt to resolve issues. But once you are indifferent, the anger and therefore the will to do anything, evaporates. Sadly, the passion about many other things goes also, and you can find yourself shrugging your shoulders at life. Who cares? Not me.

Often partners start their relationship feeling absolutely like soul mates, very connected, warm and loving. If one starts to dismiss or judge the other, or can't be bothered maintaining connection or closeness—that is, is indifferent and disengaged—emotional intimacy may be eroded and the Housemate Syndrome sets in. Once this happens, one starts to fear expressing thoughts or feelings to the other for fear of being put down, misunderstood, criticized or perhaps even let down. It may be in non-verbal rather than verbal communication, for example, the irritable or sarcastic tone, or the roll of the eyes. These expressions communicate disregard and the receiving partner will withdraw and shut down on warmth and openness, in order to protect himself or herself.

Are you living together like housemates? Feel taken for granted and not really in a loving relationship? What happens when you blame your partner for what happens to you—nothing!

When women talk about feelings men hear it as complaining. When men try to offer suggestions, women get irritated as they don't realise that he is trying to help her. As a result, one partner may simply shut down to prevent further conflict, believing that keeping quiet will help to calm things down. Any partner who needs discussion and immediate resolution of an issue will tell you this method absolutely does not work.

Level 1—Deepest intimacy

Do you remember when you first got together with your partner, when you started your relationship and were "in love"—when you were experiencing limerence? Do you remember what you used to talk about? You talked about everything, right? You couldn't get enough of each other. You got together whenever you could. You talked long into the night and were forever on the phone whenever you were not together. You would talk about yourselves and your past relationships, your hopes and your dreams, your disappointments and your failures—everything!

That was because you believed that your partner wanted to know everything about you—hungered for more! "Tell me more", is what it used to be like, "I want to know more about you." You felt safe that no matter what you said, your partner would love you and not judge you.

Level 2—Shallower communication

Then something changed somewhere along the line. Love waned and it probably started like this: She brings up a topic she wants to discuss and he retorts, "Not tonight dear, I'm tired." The negative response is different to what she is used to. "OK", she thinks, "I'll leave it till later and we'll talk before midnight!" But when she raises the topic again his answer is, "Oh, don't be so ridiculous". This second negative response causes her to decide not to raise that particular topic again. She decides that she will be more careful from now on, choose carefully what she says and when so as not to get a negative response again.

A few days later, he notices a difference in her and enquires, "Are you OK?" "Yes", she answers sharply. "Are you sure, you seem a bit different?" he persists. "Yes, I'm OK", she barks back. He also is a little taken aback by her negative response. From now on he also becomes selective about asking, about speaking, lest there is a negative response. And so begins a decrease of intimacy—of telling each other what is going on inside of head and heart—because now there is the risk of a negative response.

Level 3—The bedroom

Soon difficulties in the bedroom begin. She is now harbouring resentments against him—hurts that haven't gone away because of his earlier negative responses. He is also feeling some confusion and resentment, noticing that she is slightly distant and starting to snap and bicker more. Her short sarcastic responses really hurt. They are intended to hurt, of course. Both are starting to feel that the relationship is not as deep and connected as it used to be.

Soon he approaches her for sex, just to get back the intimacy that he feels is going astray. He is seeking reassurance that this relationship is still OK. He wants to feel close again in the way he knows how. But she is feeling the distance too, and so is not responsive to his approach. She wants to sort the issues out as she knows how. She wants to talk about the hurts, the way she feels when he snaps at her, before she feels ready for sex. So she says, "No, not tonight".

Several more answers of, "No, not tonight", and he stops asking because he doesn't like to be rejected. She notices that he stops asking and starts to feel more hurt, even more rejected than she did before. Now she feels she has the evidence that he doesn't find her special any more. She interprets his action of avoiding sex as, "He doesn't find me desirable or attractive because he doesn't want to have sex with me anymore". Soon her inner voice asks loudly, "What is happening, is there someone else?"

Level 4—Housemates

As housemates there is no emotional intimacy in the relationship any more. Neither he nor she is talking about feelings, only about things like money, holidays, and the kids. It is no longer safe to talk about feelings, about themselves, as there is too much risk of a negative response. She feels that she is walking around him on eggshells. He rehearses things in his head that he would like to say to her, but then never says them in case she goes hysterical. There is no sex and a decreasing level of trust. Resentments, suspicion, and confusion are rising, as the petty arguments and the bickering increases.

The Housemate syndrome has arrived!

Choose not to be a victim of the Housemate Syndrome

Partners need to recognise that they have become merely housemates when they start to feel insecure, unfulfilled and empty. Often they yearn to get back to that deep place of intimacy they had at the beginning of the relationship but don't know how to get there. This is where counseling can help. Counseling teaches an effective communication model (Chapters 5.3, 5.4, 5.5) enabling couples to talk to each other about the things that hurt. The model creates a safe environment where each person feels heard and understood by the other, resentments disappear, and a reconnection is made. Counseling facilitates this process in only a few sessions and insecurities about the relationship begin to evaporate as effective communication begins.

Do not fall victim to The Housemate Syndrome—get help for your relationship soon.

- **Q & A—Why Won't He Talk To Me?**

QUESTION: *My husband is happy to talk about everyday things, but he won't talk to me about his feelings. I feel we scarcely communicate, yet he tells friends we talk all the time. We never seem to be able to resolve things, and I always seem to be the one saying, "we need to talk". He rarely gets mad about things, but shuts down when he is upset so I know he does get down sometimes, about family or work. So why won't he talk to me?*

ANSWER: There are several reasons why he may not be talking to you as you wish he would. Firstly, he may not know what he is feeling. Many people have feelings but do not know the words to describe them. You only know what to call a feeling if you've learned what to label the sensation. If you do not have emotional vocabulary, you will not be able to talk about your feelings. You will also not be able to think about them (we think in language) and so you will not be able to reflect on emotional things.

Secondly, he may know what he is feeling but be fearful of judgment if he speaks. You are only "safe" to express your feelings is you learned in your family that it is OK to do so. Was your husband brought up in a family where he was told, 'Don't be so silly', 'Pull yourself together', 'stop exaggerating', 'don't go on and on about things'? If so, he will keep his feelings to himself. Or perhaps he feels judged by you? Perhaps he feels criticized or pressured to talk when he is not ready, and so shuts down to avoid further confrontation. This would suggest he is more avoidant than you.

Thirdly, he may be a person who does not need to communicate as much as you do. Some people need to communicate in order to feel loved and connected. Others feel quite happy in the marriage without saying much. He may feel sufficiently loved by you because of things you do for him, and the physical affection you give him.

Fourthly, he may be more of an introvert, happy with his own thoughts and reflections, not needing to often talk with others. Extroverts socialize to relax. The introvert is happy to socialize but finds it draining—he relaxes by being alone to "recharge".

Finally, he is a male. Women process their feelings by talking. Men work things out in their head and only speak if something is worth saying. He may genuinely have no negative feelings to discuss as he has it all sorted.

You will feel emotionally safe with a person if you can talk about your ideas, feelings and opinions without being judged. If you want someone to share their thoughts with you, be very careful not to give a negative response, or a put down or scorn, or even something as simple as "Oh don't be ridiculous". The speaker may not feel safe enough to attempt to open up again. Once a person no longer shares inner thoughts and feelings, he or she starts to communicate at a superficial level, and intimacy is reduced. For someone to have emotional intimacy with you they must be able to trust your responses. This does not mean you must agree with everything they say. But if you have a difference of opinion or some guidance and advice you wish to pass on, express it in a non-attacking and a non-blaming way. Use moderate tones. Do not put the other person down, nor tell them to grow up. If you do, it may well be the last time you are approached.

Perhaps the biggest stressor for most people in their lives is their unmet expectations—like it or not, we expect others to do what we want, when we want them to do it. We expect to have our needs met before meeting the needs of others. We expect to be loved before we give love. We live in an age where we have been taught to expect entitlements—they are our right! When we don't get what we expect our response after the event is often inappropriate—anger or anxiety, depending on your emotional style. It's all part of the "tyranny of shoulds" we are conditioned with from when we were young.

7.4 Unmet Expectations

An expectation is something that we thought would happen, or the way we imagined things would be. Or the way something "should be". It is not necessarily something that we consciously think about. Yet if our expectation is not met, it results in us experiencing a negative emotion that we then often attribute to someone else. We will feel either disappointed, or irritable, or resentful (angry) depending on the importance of the thing to us that we thought should or would happen.

For example, think about your reaction if your husband doesn't remember your birthday. Disappointed, right? Maybe even a bit irritable or sarcastic. You have a pretty high expectation that he would at least remember your special day and acknowledge it with a greeting. If he doesn't send you flowers to the office on your birthday you probably won't be disappointed because he has never done that, and therefore that is not your expectation.

Consider the different intensities of your reactions depending on what your expectations are. Example: you are sitting at the breakfast table with your family. Your 16 month old knocks over her cup of orange juice. What is your reaction? What do you say to her? If your 6 year old son knocks over his orange juice, is your reaction the same? Of course not, because you have different expectations of their abilities to get through breakfast without making a mess. Yet neither one deliberately knocked over the juice. What is your reaction when YOU knock over the juice (or the wine)? Annoyed, irritable, right? You would not expect a sensible grown up to knock over anything. But we do!

The negative emotion that you experience is a stress response. Adrenalin is felt in your body as a response to how your brain perceived the situation. No one else feels this emotion but you. Yet it seems as though someone else has caused you to feel this emotion by his or her action, lack of action or words. You say, "You made me feel…" or 'you upset me when…..". In fact what you should be saying is "I felt unimportant when..(for example).. you forgot my birthday." 'Unimportant' is the feeling, or the label you give to that particular sensation of arousal.

We have an expectation about how a relationship with a partner should be. If the partner becomes ill or suffers a disability, our expectation of what he or she will do or contribute to the relationship, will change, possibly with some resentment, but one is usually not blamed for illness or injury. If things are different to your expectation and there is choice involved, then blame often occurs. For example, the wife of a man who travels for work, complains, "You are working all week and home only on the weekend, and yet you choose to go and play golf with your mates."

Many arguments occur because we blame our partner for our expectation not being met. When we blame we complain, and our comments start with "You…". Hear how we speak, "You never spend any time with…", "You are always…", "You never consider what I might want…", "You're away all week…." and…."It's alright for you,…".

The husband at the receiving end of this blame tunes out or gets defensive, believing that he cannot be blamed for any of the above. It is not his fault he is away from home so often, working hard for the family, earning money, not even enjoying it necessarily, but tolerating it without complaint. He too has an expectation of a supportive wife, a partner who understands how it is for him being away, a team player (while he's away she will manage the running of the household), and a person who copes with the loneliness of their separation as he has to, for the greater good of working together for the family's future. So of course he will get defensive when he is criticized for not being involved with the children, only off to have a good time, loving every minute of being away, and not taking on responsibility for any family duty even when around on the weekends. And of course he will become irritable and resentful, because HIS expectation of how it will be also is not met.

The seven deadly habits of a marriage[18] that will eventually kill the relationship, are blaming, criticizing, explaining and complaining, nagging, threatening, punishing and bribing or rewarding in order to control. These externally motivated habits are deadly because, given enough time, their persistent use kills any marriage. The couple may not divorce; just stay together in a joyless relationship with no idea of what went wrong or how to revive it.

Manage your expectations—that is, manage your response after an emotional event—by not engaging in the seven deadly habits above. Replace them with seven internally motivated caring habits[19]—supporting, encouraging, listening, accepting, trusting, respecting and negotiating differences. And drop the "you" word, replacing it with "I". These strategies will reconnect you with your partner. Left to fester, unmet expectations will lead to a build up of resentments, which cause further emotional pain that will need to be resolved.

7.5 Resolving Resentments

Resentments are old hurts—emotional wounds from the past— that have never been resolved. When you think of an incident in the past and it still "hurts"—that is, your body experiences a pain—it means the brain still interprets the incident as a threat, and your body surges a stress response. It may subside in time but any pain at all still means it is an unresolved resentment. You need not think about it often, perhaps not for months at a time, but when something triggers the memory, the pain is re-experienced. This may result in you feeling overwhelmed or angry, depending on whether you have an avoidant or reactive emotional style, respectively. If the memory of the incident is purely intellectual—your brain remembers, but there is no associated pain in the body—this means the matter is resolved.

Some people recall an event so vividly that it is almost as though the event is reoccurring. Certainly the emotion that is generated is real, resulting in the memory of the event being re-experienced as if it were happening in the present tense. This is because the picture in the brain, whether a memory or current reality, will cause the body to have a stress response, and this is what is experienced as the emotion.

When an upsetting event has been resolved, it can be recalled to mind later without the body generating the same strong emotion. You might remember the incident well, and remember that you were upset or angry about it at the time, but your body does not feel that emotion now. This means that the matter has been resolved and you have moved on. Good. For your continued emotional health and well-being, this is how it should be. If the event is not happening now, it is not present tense. Things only happen in the present tense. Anything that is stored in the brain as a memory is a fantasy; it is not reality.

In other words, resentments are fantasies that continue to cause us pain and make us suffer. It is common for a person to dwell on resentments and continue his or her own suffering. If you are feeling the pain of an old hurt, it is you and only you who is experiencing the pain, because you are the only one continuing to think of it. Even after the "sorrys" have been said and the behavior of a loved one has changed, the memory of a past deed can keep the pain alive. But you are doing it to yourself, not the other person. You are being a victim.

If, however, an emotional pain keeps reoccurring in the present tense (for example, you repeatedly feel put down), there is a possibility that you may experience a physical reaction of traumatic proportions, that is, a whole body reaction—nausea, quivering, and a need to run away. This is a post traumatic stress response and is the reason you may withdraw and remain silent and not engage in the relationship. A person will do anything to avoid such a hideous and painful response. You can become "allergic" to another person, when even the thought of that person or the mention of his or her name can produce in you an intense physical response. This can result in a bewildering aversion to a person that you at one stage felt close to. Understandably this is not a healthy situation to find yourself in and often medical or counseling help is required to settle such a reaction.

- **Q&A—Resolving Past Hurts**

QUESTION—*My wife is always bringing up issues from the past that I believe should stay there. It's starting to affect our relationship, as I become angry when she brings up issues I have already apologized for and I thought were now resolved. My friends tell me women tend to do this. Why?*

ANSWER—Past hurts (resentments) are the most common cause of relationship breakdowns. As past hurts are repeatedly mentioned—particularly during conflict—the original pain is re-experienced. Even an issue you thought was resolved and well and truly dealt with can be resurrected during conflict.

This is because when feelings conflict, the brain remembers occasions from the past when the same pain was experienced—feeling let down, for example. It's much the same process that occurs when you identify a smell, your brains races through its store of memories to identify when it last experienced that particular sensation.

Typically it's the woman who's accused of "bringing up the past". But this is because women have a larger *hippocampus*—the area of the brain that stores memories to which an emotion is attached. This is the reason women remember all those important dates: a first kiss, anniversary, birthday and so on.

But men also bring up past resentments. And unlike women, who tend to try and resolve issues along the way with the often dreaded words "We need to talk", men will store past hurts until they can't take it anymore. They'll often say nothing, but suddenly "blow their top" startling their spouse with a previously unaired grievance that has built up over time.

Resentments are not about actual events or incidents that happened in the past, they are about the feelings experienced at the time of the event. The key to keeping past events in the past, is learning how to resolve present tense issues, every time. This is best done through effective communication, which we explored in Chapter 5. Sometimes you may come across difficult people or behavior that is out of your control. How do you handle these situations?

7.6 Handling Difficult People

We want to understand people; why they behave the way they do. Difficult or different behavior to our own can be a source of stress if we do not take the time to understand and manage it. Difficult people require special attention if we are to avoid emotional pain down the track when their behavior overwhelms us and keep our relationships on track.

A person's behavior is driven by a need to feel better. When the behavior is inappropriate and impacts others in a negative way, we call it difficult behavior. But behavior is almost always a means to an end, and if you can understand this in your partner/parent/child you may have a different way of managing your frustration.

The Myers-Briggs Type Indicator is an instrument that has been used for some years now by psychologists and by organizations to allow people to find out their preferred style of operating. This instrument helps organizations to find out about their staff, their different patterns of behavior, their needs, their strengths and their limitations.

The MBTI, as it is affectionately known, has been based on the personality theory of Carl Jung—a psychiatrist in the 1920s (already that is the last century, the last millennium!). This instrument identifies people's preferences in the way they deal with the world. Researchers have identified that there are different behaviors—or we can call them different personality traits—for four different dimensions that do impact specifically on relationships. These dimensions are different ways in which people prefer to deal with their world and the way that they operate.

By having some idea of these different styles, you can gain greater insight into the way that you function and the way that other people around you function. By understanding this, you are going to have greater tolerance and greater identification of the different behaviors that people exhibit, including your own, and the same information helps you to become clearer in situations where you might connect with or where you might clash with other people.

The four different style dimensions that are covered in the MBTI are firstly, whether or not you are more of an extrovert or an introvert. It also looks at whether people have a preference for being a planner, an organizer, in the way you manage your life, or whether you prefer to be an optionizer and to be more flexible and leave things open. Another style dimension is whether you are a thinker or a feeler. The fourth style dimension is big picture—whether you are a big picture person or whether you prefer to look at details.

These different styles are purely preferences. They are a natural preference. They are how you operate naturally and the style comes to you without real mental effort; it's what you do the most easily and is not necessarily permanent. Look at your natural hand for handwriting. If you are a right handed person, that comes naturally. You don't have to think about it and when writing you don't use much mental effort. But, if you are forced to write with your left hand, with concerted effort, you can do so. It might not be as good, but you can. And that's a bit like these personality styles.

The styles also are not rigid categories. It's not about you having unchanging or unchangeable characteristics. Within each style, there is a whole range of different traits, from being extreme to being half-half. Often, you can have a half-half style where you use some on one end of the spectrum and a few traits from the other end of the spectrum.

It has been researched that in a romantic relationship, it is much more likely to be successful if your styles are considerably similar. If your styles are quite different, there may be too much difference to bridge the gap. There may be considerable conflict and misunderstanding however with knowledge, this can also be overcome. Research tells us that the greatest problem in romantic relationships is when the woman is an extrovert and the man an introvert. This reportedly is the cause of many relationship problems.

Most people think that other people think the same way they do. We imagine that everybody sees the world and interprets the world as we do. This misinterpretation often leads to frustration and conflict and in fact, often because we operate differently to our partner or to people around us, we get caught up in this conflict and can lose sight of the common ground. We fight and become distressed so much about the differences that we lose sight of the things we actually still do have in common.

By looking at the different styles that impact on relationships, including rigid personalities, those with anxiety based behaviors, people who blame, narcissists and sociopaths, we can gain a greater understanding of how to handle difficult people and thereby reduce potential conflict and emotional pain. We can learn to respect the differences that exist and by doing so, we can also learn to accommodate how other people operate and to negotiate with them. We can speak out a little bit more about what's important to us because we've learnt that other people won't necessarily think of that of their own accord, because they think people in the world operate the same way they do! By accepting that one person operates differently, but with equal validity, we can be more tolerant and that too will enhance relationships. We can look at reframing these various styles as different rather than as defects and by reframing them, the differences do become more tolerable.

We turn now to learn the different ways to give and receive love and how they can help you reconnect and get your relationships back on track.

7.7 Giving and Receiving Love

Each of you has different needs that signal changes in emotions. You all have a basic need for love, affection, and esteem, but you all do not feel loved or give love in the same way. In *The five love languages*[20] Gary Chapman describes wonderfully the five different ways in which people have their need for love met; the way you give and receive love:

1. Words of Affirmation

You receive love through words of affirmation. For example, you like to be told that you look good, are competent at what you do, or have cooked a wonderful meal. "Wow! You are such a good cook, Paul. Your chilli crab was simply delicious, the best I've had in a long, long time."

People who like words of affirmation do not necessarily need praise, but they do need an absence of criticism. This is because affirmation people are particularly sensitive to tone and criticism. As kind words feel like love, harsh words and irritable tones feel like rejection.

2. Quality Time

People who receive love through quality time are those who enjoy close, deep, intimate conversation. Quality time can also just be enjoying something together, such as; riding bikes, playing tennis, or simply just sharing the Sunday paper. Many women seek quality conversation and will respond with vigor to others who take the time to be active listeners. Equally, many men need time to talk and engage fully with their partner to feel loved.

3. Receiving Gifts

Some people like to receive gifts as confirmation that they are loved. For example, a box of chocolates, a bunch of flowers, a holiday, or regular gifts of jewelry can meet a person's need for love. A husband being present at the birth of a couple's child can be regarded as a gift of his time, and will always be remembered.

4. Acts of Service

Acts of service are one sure way to express your love for someone. Cooking dinner, cleaning the house, running errands, and ensuring your partner's need for creature comforts, are all examples of acts of service that signal love. It is the simple acts of consideration that are most meaningful, although if you do ask your partner to do a task for you—such as, post the check, drive you to work—if the task is completed quickly and happily, that still signifies love. If you are an acts of service person and your partner is reluctant, or fails to do a task you have requested, you will feel unloved and a little resentful.

5. Physical Touch

Giving and receiving love by physical touch includes hugs, body massages, back rubs, holding hands as you walk in the park, stroking, and sexual intercourse.

The ways of giving and receiving love above can also be a trap. **A TRAP** is an acronym to remember the five ways of giving and receiving love—Affirmations, Time, Receiving gifts, Acts of Service, Physical touch. You may think that you are doing everything necessary to love your partner, and yet you've become "trapped" in a way of responding that does not meet his or her need at all! If you are not giving love to your partner according to his or her needs, you may end up apart.

A male client recoiled in a counseling session when first being made aware of the ways to give and receive love, "I thought I was doing everything right. Now I discover that I've been doing it wrong for the last 15 years!" He had fallen into the "trap" of thinking his way of loving his wife met her need without ever asking her how she liked to receive love. They had come to counseling because they had grown 'apart'— they were not giving and receiving love according to their individual need for love.

In order for your partner to feel loved, you need to love according to his or her needs, not your own. Chapman argues that whilst we all experience each "love language" to some degree, individuals typically have one 'primary' and one 'secondary' "love language"—be it affirmations, quality time, gifts, acts of service, or physical touch.

If you don't know which one of the five ways to give and receive love is your most preferred, ask yourself, "What have I most often requested of my partner?" That will most likely be your *primary* "love language"—the way in which you most like to receive love.

Communicate your need to your partner and others, especially your children, so that they can meet your need for love. But remember, the way you give love to others is typically the way *you* like to receive love—which means the way that *you* give love is not necessarily the way your partner *receives* love. For example, if you like to perform acts of service for people, it is highly likely that your *primary* way of receiving love is through acts of service, but this may not be the primary "love language" of your partner.

Not knowing your partner's primary and secondary "love language" can be a major reason why your relationship is experiencing difficulties. You need to "speak" your partner's love language when telling him you love him, otherwise your expression of love will fall on deaf ears. Many couples with whom we have shared these five ways of giving and receiving love in our clinical counseling practice have been amazed at how reflective of their needs the "love languages" are. Why not work out yours and your partner's "love language" today? While you're about it, work out each of your children's "love language"—you'll be glad that you did!

- **Case Study—Words of Affirmation**

    Situation: Rick and Rachel had been in a loving relationship for three years. Mostly they got along really well. They shared a love of redecorating houses, dining out and travel. They came to counseling because often when they were out with friends, Rick would 'stir' Rachel about things that had occurred in their relationship in front of the other people. For example, Rachel had struck her elbow against the car door one day as they were removing some goods they had bought. Rick teased her that "he couldn't take her anywhere because she always injured herself." He then joked with their friends that they should watch out when they walked past Rachel as she may knock into them.

    Rachel said that on most of these occasions when Rick teased her she would laugh along with him and the others as she knew he was teasing in good fun and he was good fun to be with. But recently, Rick had been going on with his teasing for too long and she had felt humiliated in front of their friends. She had asked Rick to be mindful of how she felt but once he started teasing her, he seemed to not be able to stop. When she told Rick, "That's enough," he would say, "Why, what's wrong. I'm only teasing, Rachel. It's no big deal." She felt increasingly annoyed with him on these occasions and wondered why she could tolerate it for a while, but then become resentful when he did not stop. He said he thought she was being a bit "over the top."

Work Done In Counseling: Susan discovered that Rachel's primary way of receiving love was words of affirmation; and in her case this meant an absence of criticism, rather than words that affirmed her. Rachel explained to Susan that as a child her mother had always put her down, and belittled her, telling her she was hopeless. It seemed that now when the teasing went on too long, Rachel started to have old emotions stir up that left her with the same feelings she had had back then—feelings of being put down and belittled. Rachel described that she would start to have anxiety in her chest, and it was then that she would ask Rick to stop. If he didn't, her heart would start to pound, and her body would feel drained and heavy, at which point she would start to shut down and feel very angry toward him. Typically they would argue and have tension between them for days.

Susan explained to them both that whilst loving teasing is ok, when it goes on too long it was being interpreted by Rachel as' "Rick thinks I'm hopeless". This would result in her feeling belittled and humiliated. When she asked Rick to stop and he did not, she would then feel devalued and disrespected. Each time he teased her, her nervous arousal would increase and her stress level would rise to 7 or 8 on her anxiety scale.

Whilst she was trying to reduce her stress by applying the cognitive-behavioral techniques she had learned in counseling, his continual teasing meant that in her brain she no longer saw it as funny, but now interpreted it as criticism. With each teasing her body became more aroused with adrenalin, rising to a point where she did not see it as funny anymore—she just felt exhausted. At this point she felt that Rick was not meeting her need for love and just wanted to remove herself from his presence so his now 'perceived' criticism stopped, and she could calm down. Whilst Rachel recognized she had more work to do on managing her own nervous arousal, Rick could best help her by refraining from teasing her, as this had become a major stressor for her. Rick's teasing meant that he was now not meeting her need for affirmation.

Susan's Advice For Moving Forward: Paradoxically, we only receive love after we first give love—it is in giving that we receive. Because Rachel's need for love was not being met, Rick would in turn begin to feel his need for love was not being met as stress increased and they each began to avoid each other. Rachel now must work harder on managing her response after her incorrect perceptions of Rick's teasing and Rick must work harder on minimising his teasing so as to retain his sense of humour but be more mindful of the impact of his behavior on Rachel. In this way they can each expect to receive love in the manner they need it the most. And trust can be restored.

7.8 Sandcastle of Trust

Building your sandcastle of trust, is building special relationships based upon an identity that values trust as foundational to social behavior. For many people, trust lies at the heart of relationships in the home and in the workplace. Dr Rosie King, sex therapist and educator, says,

> We all start out as trusting individuals—it is life that teaches us not to trust...When you enter into a relationship you enter into an agreement. Infidelity, lying, (and) breaking of promises...are common examples of breaches of contract... the price of betrayal is loss of trust.[21]

Dr King describes the sandcastle of trust, to explain to couples how trust can be built and destroyed in a relationship.

> In clinical practice I use the sandcastle model of trust to explain to couples how trust can be built and destroyed in a relationship.

Imagine that your trust in your partner is built like a sandcastle on the seashore, using beach sand and a spade. Trusting types possess fi equipment to rapidly build sizeable sandcastles—a good-sized emotional spade and firm damp sand to work with. Each time your partner turns up at the agreed time, you pile sand on your castle. Each time your partner is there for you, each occasion your partner tells you the truth, each time your partner places commitment to the relationship over attraction to another—on goes another spadeful of sand.[22]

Learning to trust is one of life's most difficult tasks—Isaac Watts.

The husband who goes out drinking with friends and comes home late night after night, despite assurances to his wife that, "I'll be home early tonight," will eventually lose the trust of his wife, as she stops asking where he has been—convinced that he will lie anyway.

The woman who never tells her husband how she spent her day, who she has been with or where she has been, will lose the trust of her husband as he becomes suspicious that she is seeing someone else.

An employee who "moonlights" or slanders their employer, and does not show integrity, loyalty, and commitment to his or her job, workplace, superiors, and subordinates, will lose the trust of their employer.

An employer who does not honor agreements with staff, does not pay staff legal entitlements, reneges on commitments made to employees, and does not behave toward staff in a way that respects and honors their rights, will lose their employee's trust.

As trust begins to fade, the sandcastle is demolished and needs to be rebuilt, spade-by-spade. Sometimes the pain from hurts—verbal, physical, sexual, and emotional abuse—is too severe, and the sea of time washes the sandcastle out to sea, never to be rebuilt.

Trust is a choice. We all know the cost of broken relationships on the parties concerned, particularly children. A feeling of betrayal is an emptiness—like a bag that has dropped out of your soul; like the wind was sucked out of your lungs. If your sandcastle of trust is beginning to slip away, try implementing the lessons you have learned from this book to rebuild trust. You may be surprised at what happens in your life and relationships.

- **Case Study—Infidelity: The Discovery**

    Situation: Fran had noticed that Prem was more irritable, spent less time with her and was often on his hand phone, sometimes late at night. Prem had told her that a large project he was supervising overseas meant that he needed to spend more time away from home. Fran trusted her husband and tried to support him in a stressful job.

    One day, after chatting to friends about her relationship with Prem, her suspicions were aroused that there may be a third person in their relationship. After reading Prem's emails, and finding some personal ones from an unknown woman, she experienced tremors of her lips and hands, nausea, profuse sweating, and rapid breathing. Fran later confronted Prem about her findings and he confirmed that it was true; he had been unfaithful. She called Susan in desperation as she felt immense weakness in her body and thought she was going crazy.

    Susan's assessment: Fran was experiencing an immediate emotional trauma—an emotional aftershock (stress reaction) precipitated by the discovery that Prem had betrayed her. Her shock and disbelief at Prem's infidelity was too powerful for her to manage by herself.

    Work done in counseling: Susan helped Fran to understand the physical impact of her trauma on her body. Fran experienced fully the pain of the betrayal and as the stress reaction passed, decided to receive relationship counseling with Prem to restore her marriage.

Outcome: By not trying to fight her recurring thoughts, dreams, and flashbacks of the discovery, Fran was able to maintain as normal a schedule as possible. She was willing to believe Prem when he said he wanted to recommit to her and through couple counseling came to accept and understand what had happened. Fran made the decision to trust and began the long road back to rebuilding her trust in Prem.

Susan's advice for moving forward: Experiencing a traumatic event, such as the discovery of infidelity, will cause you stress—negative emotion felt in your body. The signs and symptoms from a stress reaction (Chapter 1.6) may last for a few days, a few weeks, or a few months, and occasionally longer, depending on the severity of the traumatic event. Often the traumatic event is so painful that professional assistance from a counselor may be necessary.

When infidelity occurs, you cannot wait for the feeling of trust to come back. The reason it never will is because you will always have automatic suspicious thoughts. This occurs even after you have made the decision to trust. It is crucial if the relationship is to be rebuilt after betrayal—if you are to reduce your stress after this emotional event—that the victim of infidelity makes the decision to trust again. Otherwise rebuilding simply will not occur, and the victim of the betrayal will always blame his or her partner for the breakdown.

7.9 Trauma of betrayal

Discovering that your partner has been unfaithful in your relationship, even in just an emotional sense, can cause you to feel devastated. Often there have been signs and observations of things not being quite right, but you usually push the suspicions away, refusing to believe that your partner would stray. Even if there have been some suspicions, it is common to tell yourself that you are being silly, or overreacting. You berate yourself for being so insecure that you would even THINK such things. You tell yourself that your partner is an honest person and would not cheat on you. And you have a really good relationship. Well, pretty good anyway.

When the discovery is made, or your partner confesses to having been unfaithful, you feel shocked and devastated. Even if you had some suspicion, when you are finally told you experience a trauma reaction. It is similar to knowing that the volcano may erupt, that the signs have been there, there has been talk of possibly having to evacuate your home—but when it really happens it is still traumatic and you still must deal with your emotional response after the event.

Typically, you enter a phase of shock and disbelief, and emotional pain that is so intense you wonder if you can ever recover from it. The pain is physical, as with the discovery comes a realization of a very real threat—you and your life as you know it is threatened. By the incidence of betrayal, and in response to the threat, your body produces vast amounts of the stress chemical adrenalin. Your brain reacts to the fear by having you alternate between wanting to discover more information and wanting to run away and never think of this again—this is the fight or flight response. Initially, intense waves of feeling course through your system several times a day as you alternate between, "I love him" and "I hate him".

During the initial days following discovery, it is common to experience the full range of trauma reactions. You may tremble and quiver and be totally unable to think straight. You cannot eat. You cannot rest. The only thing on your mind is the infidelity. You may be uncharacteristically angry and pummel your partner. You may wail and sob, or both. The emotions come in waves, and fluctuate in intensity. Sometimes the brain seems to switch off the thought of the threat and allows you a few minutes of respite, and then it surges back again.

You check bank accounts and phone records and his wallet for any incriminating evidence. You search clothing and his toiletries bag, things you have never done before. You ask questions—you want to know everything and drive your partner to frustration with the intricacy of the questions you ask. As a person experiencing the pain of betrayal, you are trying to make sense of what has happened. The picture doesn't make sense, and more information is needed to make the pieces of the puzzle fit together to make a clearer picture. So even though the information may be painful to hear, and the betrayer certainly feels uncomfortable to answer so many awkward questions, it is still better for him to do so rather than you having to guess or imagine bits of information, to complete the picture.

It takes at least six weeks for the trauma feelings to subside—possibly 10 to 12 weeks. During the trauma phase, your thinking is impaired and it is really not possible, and certainly not wise, to make life altering decisions during this phase, especially if other people (like your children) will be affected by that decision. If you make a decision today to leave, you will change your mind again tomorrow and you will feel foolish and fickle for always changing your mind. Hence it is better to say, I will NOT MAKE a decision at all for the next 10 weeks and then I can have these fluctuations many times during the 10 weeks and still feel normal.

It is also normal to have fluctuations of feeling that you are coping okay—that life is returning to normal—and feeling devastated. You will often experience intense pain as you flash back to the trauma of the initial discovery. Believe that these feelings in time will pass as your brain becomes aware that life goes on even if you have to adjust to a new situation.

In the final chapter we look at emotion as the force of real life and how happiness leads to a less stressful life before we draw this book to a close.

8
Achieve Lasting Happiness — And Give Happiness To Others

8.1 Introduction

"To me it seems that to give happiness is a far nobler goal than to attain it: and that what we exist for is much more a matter of relations to others than a matter of individual progress: much more a matter of helping others to heaven than of getting there ourselves."—Lewis Carroll

Happiness is defined as the quality or state of being happy. We want to be happy, don't we? We want to be delighted, pleased or glad over someone or something. We want to experience pleasure, contentment and joy. Many of us spend our lives seeking happiness from success. In Western culture, the commercial world has conditioned us to think that we only get happiness from success; often judged by the amount of financial wealth we have created. Does success of this kind lead to happiness? It can—and there is plenty of evidence to support the notion that happy people are highly productive and seem to have a disposition to become even happier.

But success of itself may not lead to us achieving or giving lasting happiness.

Recount the many reasons that make you glad. The things that make life beautiful are not things at all—they are people, the people you know and work with, those whom you love and those who have loved you. Good relationships empower you to love and to be loved by others. They fill you with happiness and positive emotions. They are what life is about. When you forge strong and enduring relationships with those around you, when you heal emotional wounds and rebuild relationships that are broken, something real and good persists—lasting happiness. Emotion is the force of real life because in recognizing, expressing, using, understanding and managing emotion you will be empowered to create a stress free environment where you can give happiness to others.

8.2 Emotion—The Force Of Real Life

We believe that emotion matters—that emotion is the force of real life! Without emotion there is no life; simply an empty vessel moving through unchartered waters. Emotions affect social behavior—they intoxicate us so that we engage fully with life. Emotions influence a wide range of real-life situations— they can build us up and they can drag us down. Emotions can help us sustain happy, harmonious, fulfilling relationships or poor quality relationships. We get to choose. We have all been blessed with an emotional brain to manage and control our emotions—so they work for us and make us happy, not we work for them.

Traditionally, emotions were viewed as chaotic and immature—they got in the way of rational decision making. Emotions were thought to cause a complete loss of cerebral control and had no conscious purpose. Research[23] has now shown that emotions are functional and adaptive—not chaotic and harmful to logical thought.

The contemporary view is that emotions arouse our thinking and motivate us; they direct our attention to stimuli in need of processing. Emotions convey information about relationships. Each emotion signals a different relation; between a person and a friend, a family, the situation, a society, and internally between a person and his or her memory.

Researchers have argued that emotions evolved for their adaptive value in managing fundamental life tasks—an emotion may be vital to survival of the species whether in a social, biological, or psychological context. It is recognized that a thorough thinking through of emotions and emotional skills on the part of the individual may be an important source of coping.

Emotional skills are one of a broad spectrum of skills that everyone has in varying levels that are differentiated from technical skills—like accounting, business planning, and engineering—and cognitive abilities—like analytical reasoning. Many of us spend years gaining knowledge and qualifications in the "technical" skills, but too few of us spend any time at all in learning emotional knowledge, improving emotional intelligence, or enhancing our interpersonal skills. This book provides you a pathway forward to enhance your emotional skills, find emotional balance, and give lasting happiness.

8.3 Conclusion

This book teaches you how to reduce your stress after an emotional event. Our goal has been to help you manage your response to an event —your stress or negative emotion— and empower you to create and maintain more meaningful relationships every day of your life. In short, this book teaches you how to attain and give happiness—how to check your mood, balance your good and bad feelings, and give up holding on to appearances of anger or anxiety and choose instead to live in present moment reality.

Happiness is an emotion state—a state of well-being you can achieve without financial wealth. Much of the unhappiness that comes from dysfunctional relationships is avoidable. It is never one incident that wrecks a relationship—it is your inability to share and manage the feelings about the incident. For example, why is it that some couples break up following the death of a disabled child, and other couples do not? Why do some couples split after infidelity, and other couples stay together? These events evoke a myriad of negative emotions, and each of the couple's experience of the emotions is different. If these feelings can be spoken about and validated, each person feels stress reduce and feels good about the support provided by the partner. In any interaction, if you have a good feeling, you attribute it to your partner. However, the bad event has still happened. That doesn't alter. But you get through the drama, and survive, because your feelings about the experience have been heard and understood. It is when you feel unsupported and alone, put down or misunderstood, that relationships deteriorate and unhappiness begins.

When relationships do deteriorate, one partner usually blames the other: "You make me feel like this," or "You really stress me out," or "You must apologise." However, you now know that your partner doesn't cause your stress. Your partner is trying to survive the event just as you are. It is your interpretation of what your partner says or does—the blaming, the complaining, the withdrawing from the conversation, the denial of events you know to be true, the poor communication, the accusations of wrong doing, the betrayal, the teasing and joking that give you the perception that you are not loved— that results in stress.

Stress will often spawn problems between partners in relationships and create the disharmony evidenced by behavior such as blaming, accusations, and withdrawal. Let us examine how this occurs in another common example. You feel insecure and suspicious (= stress) about your husband due to his unexplained late working hours. You accuse him of being unfaithful. He feels mistrusted and unfairly attacked (= stress) by the accusation and becomes understandably defensive, which in turn fuels your suspicion. Both you and he blame each other for feeling stressed. As you feel stress rising in your body, ineffective communication begins—it's usual to tune out and stop active listening when you are stressed. Unhappiness increases as resentments escalate. You are now moving towards being housemates. The problems that stress creates can diminish in a moment all the good work that has gone into building a sound relationship.

It is important to realize that these outward behaviors (blaming, questioning, and defensiveness) are the symptoms of stress, not the cause of stress. Let us explain that in a different way. The cause of stress is not one particular event or incident which generates negative emotion. Stress (negative emotion) is caused by your appraisal, your interpretation, your perception of the incident or event. An event does not cause your stress, your appraisal of it does. This then is often the problem—an incorrect appraisal of a situation. The negative emotion you feel is simply your body signaling that something is wrong.

Have you noticed that often your appraisal is incorrect? For example, you are in a lift and it shudders a little. In reality, the lift is coming to rest at the next floor. Your appraisal might be, "There's something wrong with the lift. I'm in danger." The result is you feel stressed. Conversely you may be running late for a meeting (reality) however, if your watch has stopped and you are not aware of the time you will not be stressed. It is important to realize that often your appraisal of an event is not reality. This can cause problems in a relationship, when fantasy replaces reality.

How you deal with or manage your response following your perception of the event is critical. Recall from Chapter 3.4 that your EAR—Identity is the identity that you have created for yourself. It is the person you want to be. EAR—Identity is the key to changing your appraisal, your interpretation, your perception of the incident or event. It is the key to you reducing your adrenalin arousal, keeping your mood steady, and improving happiness.

Understanding emotion and its source is critical to your physical and emotional wellness. It really does matter that you identify the negative emotion (stress) that you are feeling and find its cause. Once you have found the cause of your stress, using a cognitive behavioural technique, such as the 4-step cognitive framework (Chapter 3.10), on a regular continual basis will reframe your perception of the situation that caused your stress. Your new conditioned response (habit) will ultimately enable you to bring your negative emotion into balance. Successfully reducing your stress will empower you to achieve wellness, reengage in your relationships and unleash your desire to give and attain lasting happiness.

If you choose to move out of your comfort zone, and really understand and practise the principles embodied in *Relax Release Let Go*, you will have significantly reduced your stress—especially the impact on you of the emotions of others—increased your self confidence and ability to maintain mood, and improved your overall health. You will focus less on yourself and care more about what others think of themselves and what you can give to strengthen their relationships with you. You will stop blaming and complaining and build your emotional life on emotional awareness, not on the weaknesses of others. And if you are grateful to someone along the way who has brought you this far and helped fill your life with joy, you should tell them. If you have been blessed by *Relax Release Let Go*, be a blessing to others.

We hope this book helps you to understand why emotion matters. We hope it helps to make your stress free life a shared blessing that will enrich your relationships and smooth your journey to happiness, today and for all the days to come.

Made in the USA
San Bernardino, CA
21 July 2017